Learning Lessons

Learning Lessons

Jonathan Jansen

BOOKSTORM

ISBN: 978-1-928257-86-8
e-ISBN: 978-1-928257-87-5

First edition, first impression 2020

Published by Bookstorm (Pty) Ltd
PO Box 4532
Northcliff 2115
Johannesburg
South Africa
www.bookstorm.co.za

Names marked with an asterisk* in this book are pseudonyms to
protect real identities

Quote on page 189 from Heard, T: *8000 Days: Mandela, Mbeki and
Beyond*, Protea Bookhouse, Pretoria 2019

Edited by Kelly Norwood-Young
Proofread by Tracey Hawthorne
Cover design by mr design
Cover image courtesy of Gallo Images
Book design and typesetting by Triple M Design
Printed in the USA

For Zara

Contents

Introduction

The question I probably get asked most often by students is: *How did you achieve what you did?* There is an urgency to the question and more than a little self-interest. If I can figure out how he made it, the student reasons, then maybe I will know how to chart my own path. It has always been difficult to provide a simple answer for a long and complex journey, so I often leave the enquiring student with a pointer here or a caution there. Never enough to really account for the full breadth of lessons I've taken from life.

Of course, the question itself makes me uncomfortable. I do not regard my accomplishments as my own. Whatever I have achieved is through the hard work and sacrifices of family and friends. That is not even false modesty; it is a fact. I am humbled by and grateful to the many who invested love, direction, encouragement and, yes, money to make my journey possible.

Then there is the simple reality that by my own estimation, what I have achieved is not mind-blowing. I know for a fact that any number of young people reading this book can do so much more. In addition, I stretch myself by holding up scholars who have made much greater strides in their careers; they are my inspiration, my models of success. However, to the extent that my story may inspire and offer direction to generations of young people concerned with living and learning, I am happy to share my journey.

That question often posed to me has been researched before. One of my doctoral students did a study on the life histories of prominent black scientists in South Africa. How did these great men and women achieve so much in their lives, despite the hardships experienced under apartheid? Her findings were fascinating: while each scientist had a somewhat unique journey towards greatness in their discipline, there were some common threads. One that stood out was a family who invested everything they had to ensure the success of their children. Interestingly, it was not only hard-earned money that made up that support, but also the constant encouragement, guidance and moral support along the journey from school to university to a senior scientific position. What that study did not do, however, was draw out the lessons learnt by these accomplished scholars about life and learning – which could be useful to generations of students to come.

Naturally, you cannot read this book as a checklist of 'what to do' to leverage your learning for success in life. Every journey is different; every circumstance carries unique challenges, and every personality manages difficulties in various ways. However, it is possible to learn from the moves and the mistakes that others have made along their way to achieving great things in life.

That is what this book offers.

Of course, all of this raises the question of what counts as success. I certainly do not mean material wealth, although earning enough to enjoy the good life is something every human being wants and works for. More than money, success means achieving that deep satisfaction that what you end up doing in your career is exactly what gives meaning and direction to your life. For example, no teacher – whether at school or university – becomes wealthy. And yet there is nothing that gives me more fulfilment than being able to teach complex things to smart minds in ways that open up worlds of possibilities.

I have seen that definition of success so often in the lives of others – like my colleague André, who is a paediatric surgeon. You can see the joy in his face as another prem baby (whose life only a few months ago hung in the balance) now smiles and kicks and clasps the mother's finger. Or my friend Setlogane, who uses the resources of his company to bring high-level mathematics and science teaching to the rural areas of central South Africa. When you watch his face shine as the A symbols are announced at a fancy gala, you just know Seth would do this job for free. And how can I not mention my favourite psychologist, born without arms and shortened legs, entrancing her audience with a story that helps so many people see their own problems in sharp perspective? Nicky can hardly conceal the joy and success she has achieved in her vibrant career.

What I know for sure is that merely accumulating wealth for yourself is not going to give you a deep sense of achievement and success – unless, of course, you share your resources with those who have less, or target those who could lift themselves out of hardship through a carefully considered investment.

I have witnessed that kind of giving with Oprah Winfrey and how changing the lives of hundreds of girls at her Johannesburg school afforded deep meaning to her life as a philanthropist. Having seen Oprah up close and working for her over several months, I can assure you there is a sincere heart beating there and a genuine concern for the lives of others.

I suppose there is no greater motivation for writing this book than the many, many students whom I have seen make simple mistakes in their youth and never recover. They become hardened and even bitter over the course of their lives. Most times, it is because they genuinely do not know what to do in a crisis or how to manage a conflict or where to go for help. The difference, in other words, is knowledge.

In this regard, you should never underestimate the difference that knowledge makes in determining your life chances. If a young person is middle-class with savvy parents who have access to networks, that individual has a much better chance of landing the right job or earning good money than someone who is poor. For a comfortably middle-class person, a mistake need not be catastrophic for the individual because there are always resources at home to tide you over until the next opportunity comes knocking. However, for a young person from a working-class home, with parents who never had the privilege of a university education and whose family members are themselves struggling, one missed opportunity could mean the end of a chance at achieving the good life.

Needless to say, whether you are rich or poor, there is no guarantee of a fulfilled life and a satisfying career if you simply do not want to do the right thing. This means that personal determination is critical as a first step towards achieving your goals. If you sit around at home and hope for someone to come knocking at the door with a bursary for studies, or train fare for work, or an application form for university, this book will not help you. Reading the book is a solid start but then you must take action. In other words, what this book offers is a roadmap – but the journey is your own.

Let's start.

Pay attention

'I never knew that the point of a gun is that cold.'

Stanley Ndimande, a taxi driver from Benoni, was about to be hijacked as he stopped to offload the last two male passengers in his 10-seater vehicle. One man locked the doors and the other kept the cold gun to his head while Stanley's girlfriend was in a panic at the back of the taxi. 'That gun was cold,' he says again as we talk.

Stanley panicked and, in the congested traffic, simply could not find the reverse gear to get out and drive in the direction indicated by his kidnappers. In the struggle to reverse, a South African Defence Force Hippo vehicle forced its way through the stranded cars towards the stalled taxi. One soldier started to beat Stanley for holding up the traffic.

At this point, the two hijackers jumped out and one of them shot a soldier in the stomach before fleeing into the nearby bush. Stanley and his girlfriend barely survived.

You would not have noticed Stanley Ndimande in a crowd. The former taxi driver decided to save up money to embark on studies away from home in the coastal city of Durban. There, he was quiet and unassuming as he went about his work at the University of Durban-Westville, photocopying materials for the lecturers to make some money to support his undergraduate studies.

What I did notice was that he was forever smiling, always going to his next task at a half-sprint and more eager than most to learn. He paid attention to detail – to his work and most of all to his studies. I decided to employ this first-in-the-family university student as my research assistant so that he could learn real skills.

It started badly. 'Would you fetch me this journal from the library?'

Stanley panicked. 'I had no idea what a journal was and I wasn't going to tell you that I did not know,' he tells me years later.

I insisted that he study abroad but the application form asked for 'a statement of purpose'. He did not know what that was, but recalls that I helped him write one.

Over time, his confidence grew and as the country slid from apartheid to democracy in 1994, Stanley, like so many other black students, reclaimed his first name, Bekisizwe. I was so impressed with both his academic talent and his humanity that I wrote to the famous professor (and now friend) in curriculum studies, Professor Michael Apple at the University of Wisconsin: 'Michael,' I wrote, 'I have an ex-taxi driver from Benoni whom I am sending to you for doctoral studies.'

'*Send him*,' came the reply.

This ex-taxi driver is now a professor of curriculum studies at the University of Texas at San Antonio, writing his own books and critically reviewing my own in international journals. This kind of thing happens when you *pay attention*.

*　　*　　*

School was a drag. Well-meaning teachers droned on in front of the class. Lots of shouting and commands: Shut up. Line up. Give up that bubble-gum in your mouth. Asking permission to go to the toilet was more about breaking the monotony of the classroom than relieving any urgent physiological need. Some teachers would simply refuse habitual requests and every now and again, a primary school child would wet themselves in the classroom.

Acts of discipline broke the spell of boredom. Like when one primary school teacher with a temper reputation hurled a bunch of keys in the direction of a boy who was talking in class. He ducked, and the keys cut open the forehead of the boy behind him. Teachers did not apologise in those days and parents did not sue educators. In fact, if you came home with a grievance, you were likely to receive another hiding or hear 'the teacher must have had a reason to beat you'.

More than anything, I looked forward to the two breaks – the short one and especially the long break. The boys divided into two teams. Captains were chosen. The toss happened some-where during a lesson on fractions or synonyms. Team names followed the two local clubs, Hellenic and Cape Town City, or

English teams from far away. When the bell rang, we rushed out into the sand or onto the tarmac – there were no rolling green fields like at the white schools, such as Zwaanswyk High School down the road, and sometimes there was no real soccer ball. A tennis ball gave as much joy to the imagination.

It was at one of those high school soccer games – during 'the interval', as we called it – that I saw my Latin teacher leaning against one of the pillars along the corridor outside his classroom. Paul Galant was a leaner – against the blackboard as he taught or against an outside wall as he conversed with his colleagues. This time, he was watching me scramble across the tarmac in pursuit of the tennis-cum-soccer ball. 'Come here, my boy.'

I was mildly irritated. The game was in the balance – it always was. But I had no choice so I went over to where my teacher was standing. 'You know, you pretend to know nothing. But I've been watching you. You're actually very smart. You have potential. I will be looking to see how you do in the next test.'

'Thank you, Sir,' I said, half-bewildered, and hurried back to the match.

I do not fully know what happened in that brief interaction, but it changed my life forever. *I am watching you. You are smart. I will see what happens in the next test.* Nobody had ever told me that I had potential, that I was clever. Nobody.

For the first time in my life, I studied for a school test. And I studied hard. My teacher was watching me. From that moment on, I started to rise in the class, from always hovering around the class average to being one of the top three or four students in high school. I was starting to pay attention.

I had come under the influence of a good teacher. My high school had a few teachers like that, who not only taught the subject but found time to encourage you – like Mrs Akoojee, my biology teacher with the grey-blue eyes. She kept telling me, 'I am expecting an A from you in biology.' Or Mr Jooste, the geography teacher, who did not even teach me (I chose history) but whenever he saw me, would ask, 'How are your studies going?' or say, 'Good luck with the final exams.' These were salt-of-the-earth teachers who made all the difference. They were influencers who made an impact if you paid attention.

This is the one lesson about successful learning that made all the difference in my life. I responded positively to those who tried to encourage my learning and who expected much from me. Of course, I could have ignored Mr Galant and continued to be an average learner, doing well enough to pass but not working to my full potential. But I did more and I sought out my Latin teacher's help in my overall development as a young student.

As a result, when Mr Galant put out a call for athletes interested in the 800 metres (it was 880 yards before South Africa changed to the metric system in 1970), I showed up after school. As with academics, I was fairly average when it came to running. In fact, my younger brothers were much better athletes in the 200-metre and 400-metre sprints (Peter and Isaac, respectively). My youngest brother (Denzil) actually came second in high-jump at the interschool championships. I never came anywhere but I was buoyed by my Latin teacher's encouragement and so I showed up for practice regardless.

It was hard: up and down the sand dunes until your calves hurt; early-morning runs around the patchy school track, where the thorns constantly cut into your bare feet and the sand held you back. It was hell. But I showed up every morning and every night. Then came the day of trials. The school would choose two learners from every age group to qualify for a specific discipline at the interschool competition, which convened at Greenpoint Track. I still remember the flutter in my stomach that morning as a teacher fired the starting gun. '*Daar hol hulle!*' (there they go) was the refrain from the sidelines every time a distance race got underway.

The star in the under-16, 800-metre group was a chap called Alex Thomas. By some miracle, I was hot on his heels as we reached the final 200-metre bend. Then there was the sprint down the home straight. Alex won and immediately turned to me, saying, 'I was wondering who was breathing down my neck.' The last person he expected was that nerdy Jansen kid in the other English class. I felt good that for the first and only time, I was in the school team headed for Greenpoint.

The encouragement in academics had rubbed off in my performance in athletics. This was a lasting lesson about the power of a teacher's words.

It was another long hour at church. The youth normally hung about for some time, chatting, while parents were doing their own catching up. Suddenly, I saw a shy-looking chap about my age (11 or 12), standing against the wall to the side of the church building. His family were newcomers. I introduced myself, not knowing that this new friend was about to turn my life upside down.

Depending on who you spoke to, his name was either Archie or Lennie (his full name was Archie Leonard Dick). Most people called him Lennie to avoid any confusion with Archie Dick senior, his father.

We would see each other virtually every single day and the subject of conversation was mostly soccer, long before it became girls. There was, however, something different about Lennie. He was a serious student. He was also at a serious school: South Peninsula High School – a black institution in a white area that refused to be relocated under apartheid's Group Areas Act. The school had a reputation for academic excellence and the students from 'SP' carried themselves with a swagger compared to the rest of us from working-class schools like my own Steenberg High School.

Strangely, Lennie actually did his homework and studied every day. Fine, but then he also did something weirder. He would study through the night every Friday evening. This was so bizarre to me but he was my best friend, so on Fridays I would drag myself to his home on Sonata Street. At first, I just wanted to see what on earth this studious youngster was really up to.

Here was the pattern. Lennie would study for two hours and then take a break for coffee and doughnuts or some other eats his mother had prepared. Then he soldiered on for another two hours, followed by the next break. This time, he sometimes ate something and took a run around the block. Back to the books after that, before another round of eats. I watched this madness and made my decision. I would sleep, but I gave him strict instructions: *Wake me up for the breaks.*

Eventually, I gave in and joined the one-man (now two-man) study group. Initially, I dozed off around midnight but eventually I got the hang of it and became quite the student myself. I started to enjoy studying – more so, because I could discuss difficult concepts or hard-to-solve problems with him for an interesting reason. Lennie was my exact age – a month apart by birth – but he had been 'promoted' in primary school because he was deemed to be too smart for his grade. He jumped ahead by two years, thereby becoming the youngest member of the class throughout his school years. In other words, whatever I was learning, he had already mastered.

Lennie taught me a vital lesson as a high school student: application. My marks started to improve. Like him, I loved the sciences. He boasted about Mr Coker at SP and I bragged about Mrs Akoojee at Steenberg. We laughed about funny teachers like Mr Hilario, who taught Latin at both schools during his career and whose name lent itself to childish humour. '*Waar lê die ou?*' one group of students would shout from a safe distance when this teacher came into sight, to which another group responded in chorus: 'Hilario!' (*hier lê die ou*, in Afrikaans). And then there was another 'Sir' at SP called MT Wessels, whose name started a well-known proverb.

With all the serious studying going on during those Friday-night sessions, there were still lighter moments and fun competition. Somewhere in the early hours, during one of the study breaks, we would start a high-jump contest over his mother's washing line in the back yard, with an old mattress to cushion the fall. Lennie had mastered the Fosbury Flop. This would be followed with a 100-metre dash from the pavement of Mr Henry's house, the concrete bricks serving as starting blocks, straight down towards the front door of the Dicks' home. Then the 800 metres from the house, around the canal behind rows of council houses, and then along the main 'boulevard' to the same door. He usually pipped me in the sprints but I had the edge in the longer distance.

More seriously, in Lennie's little council house was a piano that was at the centre of our lives. Lennie's parents sent him to get piano lessons from a white lady on the other side of the railway line. He would come back playing pieces I had never heard before like Handel's 'Largo in G' or Beethoven's 'Für Elise'. I was mesmerised by the beautiful chords and watched as he practised with concentration for hours on end.

Then something else happened that would bring much joy into my life. I started to memorise what Lennie was doing on the piano and tried to 'play by ear'. It was a mess, of course, but I kept trying. Fortunately, around that time, we had a talented group of church youth who played various instruments, mainly by ear. I observed and learnt from them and started playing the piano with more confidence.

Lennie graduated from high school and went on to study what was then called library science at university. I had no intention of 'studying further', as people in the community used to phrase it, but since my best friend did it, I followed suit. My love of biology firmly entrenched, I did a BSc degree with botany and zoology as majors. There is no doubt in my mind that studying further might not have happened if this precocious young boy had not entered my life early on.

'How do you manage peer pressure?' a student once asked me during a high-school address.

'You choose the right peers,' I advised.

It turns out that Mr Galant had also taught and inspired Lennie when he was at a nearby primary school. After both of us gained our doctorates and professorial appointments, we decided that it was time to acknowledge the role of the great teacher in our lives. We found the Latin master's address and delivered an invitation to dinner for him and his wife. It was an emotional evening I will not easily forget. 'Thank you, Sir. You made us what we are today.'

For every good, influential teacher, I felt there was a bad one who threatened to derail me from life and learning. I still struggle to deal with a particular emotional trauma from my high school days.

One morning I was walking along the long high school corridor when I saw Mr 'Diff' Abrahams coming towards me from the other direction. *Diff* (Afrikaans slang) was his nickname because of his unusually large forehead, and helped to distinguish him from one or two other male teachers on the staff who shared the same surname.

'Good morning, Sir,' I hailed as we approached each other. Then, without warning, he gave me an almighty slap that saw me flying across the tiled floors. To say I was shocked would be an understatement. I was confused, angry and on the verge of crying. I got up, unsteady, and asked, 'Why, Sir? Why?' Another slap, this time harder. I went flying again. I dared not ask again. To this day, I have absolutely no idea why Diff Abrahams assaulted me that morning – not that there needed to be a reason to assault a child. It was wrong.

For years later, I wracked my brain to try and figure out what caused this huge man to hit me, twice. He did not teach me any subject so it could not have been something I had done in his class. I was seldom in the principal's office for making trouble. In fact, I had never even had to climb onto the outside stage at Monday morning assembly, when offenders were paraded before the school. That dishonour fell to other troublesome students including, on a regular basis, the head prefect of the school – a chap called Bobby, who was selected for his popularity as everyman's friend, rather than his good behaviour.

High school came and went, and my first-class pass meant that I could study further. It was the worst time to go to university in South Africa: 1974–1977. When 1976 exploded with the Soweto Uprisings, the protest movement spread quickly to the rest of South Africa. The University of the Western Cape (UWC) was primed for anti-apartheid resistance. Up to that point, campus protests at UWC were about local issues, such as the wearing of a tie (really) or the poor treatment of a lone black academic.

But this was something big – a national uprising.

Classes were interrupted; police chased students off the campus into the surrounding 'bush' (the shorthand name for black universities those days – the bush colleges); progressive lecturers were harassed, while students were detained alongside frequent shutdowns of the academic programme. I failed my first year in part because of the Afrikaans teaching in some classes (I could not understand formal, academic Afrikaans); in part because of the hardship of travelling in the early mornings and early evenings between Cape Town's southern and northern suburbs, using three or more forms of transport; and in part because of the academic disruptions.

One day, after leaving home at about 5.30 am on the other side of the Cape Peninsula, and rushing through the water spraying onto the campus grass to reach my chemistry lecture in time, I entered the upper back door of the science auditorium, wet and breathing heavily. The white professor of organic chemistry with a French-sounding name looked up and told me to leave his class. I was shattered. Right there and then, I decided this was just too difficult. I was still tired from the late 'labs' from the day before; I had to borrow money to take the taxi, bus and train, and I really did try to be on time. Now this. That's it. I'm done. This is too hard.

For the first time in my life, I felt defeated. I went to the campus cafeteria, which I used to avoid like the plague – that is where the lazy students like Porky from our church used to bunk classes and while away the time playing a card game called *klawerjas*.

I bought a bunny-chow (a hollowed-out loaf of bread filled with bean curry) – the comfort food I needed at that moment. Then I bought the *Cape Herald*, a trashy local newspaper that nevertheless had job adverts in the back pages. I applied for one of them.

A first-year dropout with elementary chemistry was never going to make it at Anchor Yeast, a company not too far away from the university campus. The job required me to run tests of various kinds using experimental solutions in the laboratory section of this yeast-making plant. The rather arrogant young English (as in, from England) woman technician took some joy in pointing out that I was not even holding the pipette in the right way. I had never done titrations at school and was just starting off at university. So she recommended that I leave.

Back home, I was now depressed and started to prepare myself for a life that would probably swerve between unemployment and uncertain employment, as was the case for so many men in my community.

My mother had other ideas. She must have talked to my dad's cousin, Martin Marks, who was a salesman with a car. Not long after I dropped out, Uncle Marty, a kind and generous man, spoke to me about going back to university. I had a heavy heart about all of this but gave in to my uncle's gentle influence. His little yellow Volkswagen Beetle drove me from the suburb of Retreat all along Modderdam Road to the gates of the university. I would give the degree another go.

There was one problem. Having failed my first year, there was no bursary to pay for the repeat year. The first hurdle was the registration fee – the princely sum of R20. People where I lived did not have that kind of money lying around. My parents certainly did not. This attempt to re-register could come to a quick end after all.

I was obviously embarrassed by having failed and on top of that, not having registration money, but shared this dilemma with people at my local church. These were working-class folk without discretionary money; in fact, the church was so poor, we gathered in the small garage of the James family in nearby Grassy Park.

Mr James, who worked for the Cape Town City Council, was an upright man who found a way of putting some of his children through college and university. Earnest was the clever one, an engineer, and older than me. He used to earn money during his studies through holiday internships at Murray & Roberts, the engineering firm. I am sure Mr James or his wife, Aunty Babs, must have mentioned my plight to their son because one night after the prayer meeting in the garage, Earnest called me over to his very small room (only a single bed could fit in there) and held out a R20 note. This earnest engineer-in-the-making was not known for smiling, or any sort of exuberance for that matter. He just held out the note and said nothing. The message on his serious face was nevertheless clear: Don't screw it up. To this day, whenever I address an audience where Earnest is present – such as a recent keynote to the League of Friends of the Blind – I make it a point of acknowledging his timely influence in my life.

Back on campus, things were still very difficult. Regular

protests. Disrupted classes. Student detentions. Long com-
mutes. Racist lecturers. What I did realise, however, was that for
me, this was the last throw of the dice. If I failed again, it was
over and I would probably sell snoek for Uncle Japie Solomons
on the corner of Retreat Road and Prince George Drive (the
M5) for the rest of my life. So I knuckled down. I studied hard.
I slept at a family friend's home in nearby Belhar during examinations. I had to pass.

And still it seemed as if the universe was conspiring against
me. The inorganic chemistry lecturer was one of the worst academic teachers I had ever encountered. Grobler made it a point
of demonstrating that he hated teaching us. As students, we
used to muse that the Afrikaner lecturers who could not make it
at the elite white universities like Stellenbosch were dumped on
the bush universities.

He seldom looked up from his notes. His English was really
poor when he tried to do the occasional translation from
Afrikaans for those of us who could not make any connection
between 'suurstof' and 'oxygen'. At least 'koolhidrate' was 'car-
bohydrates' but other science terms required some translation.
Grobler was a miserable man.

At one point, the majority of the science students bunked his
class for a protest action. A few students apparently showed up
for class and he dutifully went ahead and taught the decomposition of uranium. There was no reference for this in the textbooks
and those who attended took sparse 'notes' from his miserable
writing on the board. Try as I might, nobody would or could
give me those 'notes'. Then came the examination. There was

a solo question on the decomposition of uranium. We all failed and you could see the smirk on Grobler's face as he handed out the scripts with zeros in abundance.

Years later, I returned from my studies at Cornell University with a Master of Science degree under my belt. With the confidence of an American degree, I drove to the UWC campus with one intention: to confront Mr Grobler. There I saw the miserable man sitting in his office, looking down at some or other papers. No appointment – I sat down and started to give him a lecture on what a pathetic academic teacher he was; that despite his determination to fail all of us, I had made it. And I hoped to high heaven that he changed his attitude and did not destroy the life chances of other science students who had no choice but to take his miserable classes. The poor man was in shock and disbelief. As he struggled to respond, I walked out.

For every bad influence in life, however, there is a good one. Cecil Leonard was one of them for me.

The zoology lectures at UWC offered much-needed relief for a mix of reasons. Dr Leonard (before his promotion) was fluent in English. He came from the same Cape Flats community as the students. He was easily the best academic teacher in the science faculty – the lecturers who had taught high school were the ones who could break down complex concepts in ways that first-year students could understand. He was a role model when few black lecturers at the time had PhDs. And he was funny. I'll always remember one of his jokes, which had us all in stitches during a zoology class on amphibians:

Three frogs appeared before the magistrate charged with disturbing the peace. The magistrate asked the daddy frog, 'Why were you making so much noise?' to which the father responded, 'Your honour, we were only making bubbles.' Then the magistrate turned to the mommy frog. Same thing: 'We were only making bubbles.' At this point, the exasperated magistrate turned to the baby frog: 'And what do you have to say for yourself?' The little frog explained, 'Your honour, I am Bubbles.'

Whether it was the physiology of the platanna (*Xenopus laevis*, a flat frog, literally) or the marvels of human anatomy, the 'zoo' lectures were easy – not only because Cecil Leonard made the knowledge accessible, but because he was accessible as well. Dr Leonard's lectures made my life bearable at UWC, and from time to time, I went to speak to him after class simply because of the positive influence that his teaching had on my life. From him, I learnt the first lesson of academic prowess: good professors teach for connection.

I gained so much by *learning under the influence* of good people. The Latin teacher who noticed me, the school bestie who encouraged me, the random teachers who uplifted me, the mother who raised a family alert, the uncle who transported me back to campus, the engineering student who funded me, and the zoology professor who inspired my love of the biological sciences.

Over the course of my life, these influencers kept me steady and focused. Think of your own influencers as guardrails on a swinging bridge along your learning journey. As you walk along that unstable bridge of life and learning, there are forces trying to unsettle you, to throw you off course. A lack of funding. A hard commute. A discouraging teacher. Low self-esteem. Family struggles. A shortage of textbooks. A need for food. Constant tiredness.

You may also tend to notice these influencers in the rearview mirror of life. Only later do you recognise how they have all actually fitted together to make your learning and living possible.

What is scary, later, is the realisation that if any one of those influencers had not played their role, you might well have dropped out or over the sides of the swinging bridge. The influencers are not, in retrospect, random people. They form a tight and interconnected guardrail, even though most of them may not know about each other or about their influential roles in your life. 'What if?' is a question I constantly ask myself, with a heart of gratitude that they all showed up in my life and learning.

The problem, of course, is that as the receiver of these positive influences, you must be open to being influenced. *Paying attention is key to successful learning.* I could have ignored my Latin teacher completely and not recognised that special moment when he called me aside. I could have slept through the Friday nights of study that my best friend offered. I could have refused to take up the offer of my uncle and not return to university. To be influenced positively, you have to be receptive to influencers. That part is up to you alone.

Then, of course, there is the problem of the negative influences. The double slap-down by Diff Abrahams could have sent me into an uncontrollable rage and I was big enough at the time to retaliate. The destructive academic behaviour of Dr Grobler could have ended my tertiary studies.

Yet in a strange way, these negative influences also became part of the learning experience. Mr Abrahams taught me how not to relate to students. Because of him, I decided to give everything to the academic success of my students and to love them. He was one of the reasons that I visited every one of the high school students in my 'register class' in their homes. Dr Grobler taught me how not to teach. To this day, I walk around the class with a handheld mic as I teach, engaging individual students with questions and puzzles as I move from row to row.

People like Abrahams and Grobler have immense potential to cripple the human spirit and I have no doubt that there are many victims of their callousness. But if we give in to their negative influence, they win. I decided that they would not gain the upper hand in my life. And so, while positive influences teach by showing you how to be, negative influences teach by warning you how not to behave. How you take these lessons on board is also a choice you make. Nothing about you or your potential is predetermined. It really is up to you whether you pay attention to those good influences in your life.

You are smarter than you think

The first time Christina Amsterdam wore shoes was when she reached high school. She came from a small town called Hopefield 136 kilometres west of Cape Town and a full 40 kilometres from the Vredenburg school, where I would teach her high school biology for two years. I visited her family home and her parents were warm, simple, working-class folk who loved their children. If Christina passed high school, she would be the first in the family.

Christina was small, timid and uncertain of herself, even though there was every indication in her tests and assignments that she had massive potential. Her ambitions, however, matched the landscape, where young people in her town faced unemployment or low-income jobs in the fishing industry. In the *voorligting* (guidance) class, she listed secretary, teacher and nurse as her career options. She would aim to pass Grade 10 and then go and work as a business secretary somewhere, she thought.

I am hopeless at most things except two: I can spot a potential

800-metre athlete a mile away and I have learnt how to identify a potential academic star in a class full of students. Christina, despite her humble dwellings and her quiet spirit, was that student. It was important, I decided, to nurture and encourage that talent for she clearly was much smarter than she could imagine. One way I did this was to become a lifelong mentor to Christina, which has taken her through her Master's studies in the USA and her return to South Africa.

It seems like the other day that I learnt she had become a professor of education, teaching courses in education leadership and education finance at top American universities. She returned home and I had the privilege of hiring Christina during my term as Dean of Education at the University of Pretoria. For some reason, when she arrived for the interview, I looked downwards. The young woman who once wore no shoes now stood in some serious heels.

* * *

I was literally shaking as I stood in front of the door of the famous professor known to me only through his books. I was nervous and excited. This was Joseph Novak, the man who invented concept maps for representing science knowledge and who wrote ground-breaking papers on misconceptions in science education. It had been a long trip from Cape Town to an orientation session for South African students on a small liberal arts campus outside Columbus, Ohio. We had then dispersed across the USA to some of the most prestigious universities in the world and now, here I was, at Cornell University in Ithaca, New York, about to meet Joseph Novak.

The decision to leave my job in Cape Town was not an easy one. In my mid-twenties, I was a biology teacher at Trafalgar High School in District Six when another rich influence in my life, John Volmink, told me about Cornell University. John is older than me and his younger brothers were my friends from a different branch of the same evangelical church. John, and my school friend Lennie, obtained their scholarships to study in the USA from the Educational Opportunities Council (EOC) in Johannesburg. The fund was set up in 1979 by then Bishop Desmond Tutu and an American cleric and development activist called David Smock. Their vision was that South Africa would soon be liberated and that there should be a class of black leaders trained and ready to take over in government and civil society.

To be honest, for many of my generation, the notion that the apartheid government was about to collapse was far from clear in the mid-1980s. I was, however, at a point in my teaching career where I realised there were only so many ways in which you could teach the life cycle of the fern. It would be great if I could expand my knowledge of biology teaching by doing a Master's degree in the subject. So with John's encouragement I applied for the EOC scholarship and where required on the application form, I indicated that Cornell University was my first choice. By this time, John had told me about a fascinating professor called Joseph Novak and shared books written by this eminent scholar.

After I was accepted to study abroad, the Langa/Uitenhage shootings took place and I felt a deep need to stay and be with my biology students during a struggle which had already taken its toll on some of them. I was also recently married to Grace and wanted to settle down, as they say in these parts, and build a family in South Africa. On the other hand, this opportunity might never come again and, after all, South Africa's educational problems would still be around by the time I finished the Master's degree in a couple of years. After much tossing and turning, we decided to go. What convinced me was the once-in-a-lifetime opportunity to study with Joseph Novak.

Now here I was in front of the great scholar's door.

I knocked nervously and the door swung open and a short, white, smiling man with rosy cheeks stretched out his hand. 'Are you the man from Africa?' he asked. I knew instinctively that this was not the time to be political and remind him that Africa is a continent, not a country. Almost immediately, he turned around and went towards the office shelves heavily laden with books. He returned with a manuscript held together with an elastic band. 'This should have been with my publisher but I held it back because I wanted your feedback first.'

I nearly wet myself. My feedback? I am a lowly teacher from South Africa in the office of a world-renowned academic and he wants my feedback? What on earth do I know? What could I possibly say? My heart dropped but I could sense that the man was dead serious.

So I took the document back to my student apartment and sank into the cheap couch bought with my settling-in allowance.

What now? Oh my word, he is going to find out I am a complete dunce and send me back to Africa. What do I do next?

I read the manuscript several times. Many of the words made no sense whatsoever, like 'epistemology' and 'metacognition'. I was still learning to use one of the typewriters given to us as students and there was no internet to google some of these foreign words. Still, I had a deadline so I wrote and rewrote pages of comments before typing them up and leaving the manuscript and comments with the prof's secretary. Classes started and I was not sent home. In fact, Joe (he insisted, like many US professors, on the use of his first name) thanked me for the comments.

In the course of my two-year Master's degree, it gradually dawned on me what Joe was communicating since our first meeting. His message was something I had not experienced in my undergraduate studies. Joe believed that I had something to say. He was a genuine human being, as any of his students would attest. I knew he was not testing me to see whether I belonged there in the first place. Joe Novak wanted me to know that I was not simply a student but a valued colleague. For this great academic, I had something to say.

When I met with the older South African students at Cornell I told them the story. Those who had been in American academic culture for some time, like Mzamo Mangaliso (management sciences) and Jan Persens (mathematics), laughed because they had experienced the same thing. American universities take their graduate students (what we call postgraduate students) very seriously, especially if you show signs of promise. What a contrast to the UWC days.

To this day, I often ask a large audience that I am addressing to raise their hands if, during their college or university studies in South Africa, something like this happened to them: The professor introduces himself on day one and then says something like, 'Welcome to Biochemistry 127. By the end of the first semester, half of you will be gone.' Most of the hands go up, black and white, and, to my horror, older as well as young members of my audience. Here is the difference between the South African academy and the American academy: in the US universities, the professors expect you to do well.

With Joe's heightened expectations in mind, I worked harder than ever before. It was difficult. The Americans spoke very fast and very loud and came across as super-confident. In the small seminars for Master's students, often mixed with some doctoral candidates, you were easily exposed if you did not speak up. In fact, every professor started their seminar with this notice: A certain percentage of your mark will be based on classroom participation. I felt the shock go through my body when I first heard this. You could no longer hide as in a large undergraduate class. I was truly terrified.

Easily the most important lesson I learnt during this baptism of fire in American pedagogy was to overcome the fear of embarrassment. A South African student typically holds back and hesitates to ask a question in academic contexts (we show far less hesitancy in political contexts) out of a fear of appearing stupid or feeling inadequate. American students have no such qualms and I quickly learnt the language moves that express such confidence. *Let me get this straight – are you saying that if X then Y but not Z?* Or, *Could you run that by me again? If I heard you correctly, you are saying that A might be the cause of B?* I also discovered that what enabled such confidence in questioning was that the professor was very unlikely to insult you or make a sarcastic comment about your question, compared to my familiar experience in South Africa.

I was lucky to be in a two-year Master's programme (most of the Master's programmes were of one-year duration) because it gave me more time to get used to learning the peculiarities of the US academic system. One of those learnings was that you were expected to get a 4.0 grade point average (GPA) as a graduate student. Anything below 3 and you were suspect. A GPA of 3.5 and upwards put you within respectable range and I hovered in that zone during the first year.

By the second year of studies, I had started to figure out three important learnings. First, you had to speak confidently and assertively in those fast-moving seminars or you would fade into oblivion. Second, you had to do the assigned readings in advance or your ignorance would quickly become evident in the seminar discussions. Professors seldom gave long lectures in these sessions; they introduced the topic and the students took over. Third, you had to have your own views on the subject under discussion. The most common feedback from an American professor on an assignment was: 'Okay, so I now know what the author thinks but what do *you* think?'

In this new academic environment, I thrived for the first time in post-school studies. The reason was simple: the professors thought I was smart; they valued my opinion and they encouraged my voice. This was completely new to me. I had had individual teachers who believed in me back home but this was different: the entire system sent a powerful message that *you are smarter than you think.*

Before I knew it, I was invited to speak at conferences; to chair a panel; to co-author an article; to review a manuscript; to join a research and evaluation team; to talk about 'the situation back home' on campus and in the broader community. It is a wonderful, liberating feeling when everyone around you expects you to do well.

That sense of liberation was not only intellectual; it was also political. I extended my learning beyond the seminar room, especially after I was elected in 1986 as the follow-up Secretary General to Sakumzi 'Saki' Macozoma, to the student council representing South Africans studying in the US under various funded programmes. Saki's sudden departure was itself a lasting lesson in social commitment. He was a journalism student at Boston University and one day got an urgent call that he was needed back home. Just like that, he packed his bags, gave up his studies, and left for the airport, though not before briefing me on what my job as Secretary General entailed, including the fight on divestment. I have admired him ever since.

The question of US universities divesting from companies doing business in apartheid South Africa was becoming a huge movement in that country. I spoke at Cornell and other campuses, urging divestment. I debated the UCT vice-chancellor at the Yale Club in New York – I don't think Stuart Saunders ever forgave me for telling him to go back home and raise funds for black students at UCT from wealthy white South Africans, and not here in the Americas. At Cornell, I would meet giants in the global struggle against racism like Enuga Reddy from the United Nations and Stokely Carmichael, later Kwame Ture, whose anti-Semitic tirade on the Cornell campus turned me off the man.

The strangest thing was that I attended classes on South Africa by professors who had never visited the country. Easily the best of those seminars was led by Professor Locksley Edmondson from Jamaica whose lectures were as invigorating as they were informative. As the extent of my miseducation dawned on me, I quickly realised that I did not know my country. Locksley believed in the academic boycott, which explained why he had not visited South Africa. He brought into his classes activists I would never have met – like stalwarts from the Black Sash and the End Conscription Campaign, as well as some of the most impressive thinkers from the exiled African National Congress (ANC) and Pan Africanist Congress (PAC) in New York. When I think of such intellectuals and fighters as David Ndaba (his struggle pseudonym) and Henry Isaacs, it is hard to square such brilliance and integrity with the leaders of those parties today.

One man who made a mighty impression on me was a soft-spoken academic in Africana studies with Locksley who was also exiled from home. His name was Congress Mbata. *Who is this kind-natured man?* I thought, when first introduced to him. I was overwhelmed with emotion when I realised that Professor Mbata was a founder-member of the ANC Youth League. He knew the Mandelas and the Mbekis but he was so self-effacing that you had to find all of this out for yourself. Years later, I visited the Garden of Remembrance at Freedom Park in Pretoria and there, on the granite Wall of Names, was etched the name of one of our fallen, Congress Mbata. I stood there for some time, saddened by the loss of the genius of a scholar whom generations of South Africans did not have as their professor because of apartheid.

Locksley took great pride in the connection he made between his timid young South African student and this colossus of a man in Africana studies. I then understood how Locksley might have gained so much first-hand knowledge of apartheid. More than 30 years later, I was asked to speak at a Cornell Symposium in honour of Locksley's retirement. The title of my talk was 'How Locksley fought apartheid without setting foot in the place'.

Back in the late 1980s, hardly a month went by without the tall Jamaican putting me on a platform to speak about apartheid or debate some right-wing South African who felt that government reforms would be underway if only the blacks would be more patient. This political learning was as important as my academic learning at Cornell University. Both gave me a sense of competence in their subjects but, as importantly, both strengthened my confidence as a student.

The most unpleasant of those encounters, thanks to Locksley, was debating Johan Olivier, a fellow graduate student at Cornell who was employed by the Human Sciences Research Council back home. Johan would make the most ridiculous statements about apartheid reforms and then accuse black South Africans of being more privileged than whites because they were funded to study in the US. At times, my anger got the better of me, but Locksley kept putting me and this bearded Afrikaner into the ring together. I was delighted to find, years later, that Johan had changed completely and become a real champion for transformation back home. We enjoy a social media friendship today and it is hard to believe it is the same man with whom I sparred a few thousand miles from our home.

The expectation that I could do well also meant that I stretched myself academically. I took advantage of Ezra Cornell's rather unique founding statement from 1868: 'I would found an institution where any person can find instruction in any study.' The shorthand 'any person … any study' was fairly radical then, for on paper, it opened the university to students of any race, class or religious background. What is still radical today is that you can literally study anything you wish in composing your degree. While I was in science education, the degree was a MS or Master of Science qualification. Even though I was in education, my department was part of the life sciences and agriculture school. So off I went doing gender studies with Chandra Mohanty, author of the well-cited piece *Under Western Eyes*, and of course Africana studies with Locksley Edmondson. I was like a sponge absorbing everything I could possibly be interested in studying. It also helped that you could 'audit' a course in an American university, which meant attendance without the obligation to write an examination. I joined a science class.

One of the things about raising expectations is the environment in which you study. It lifts you. This was easily one of the most beautiful campuses in the world with its stunning gorges in the Finger Lakes region of upstate New York. I walked to classes down hills and across bridges, with waterfalls below me, and then collected my favourite bagel with cream cheese from the shop on the edge of campus. But the inspiration of Cornell was much more than its physical beauty: it was the array of stars that dotted the campus.

Thanks to a popular television series called *Cosmos*, South Africans knew of Carl Sagan, who was a professor at Cornell. I would point out the distinguished astronomer's home to visitors en route to our apartment. Then there was the famous developmental psychologist Urie Bronfenbrenner, and of course, Barbara McClintock who won the science Nobel for her work on the cytogenetics of maize and whose life is captured in a beautiful biography called *A Feeling for the Organism*. Being on a campus with such famous scholars and scientists made me feel that I was in the best company. Their achievements spurred me on to live up to the expectations of the institution itself. I could not have been more motivated.

It was not only the great scholars who were positively influencing my learning journey. It was also a professor of apples (pomology is the fancy title) named Robert Smock, the father of David Smock, who with Desmond Tutu, started the EOC scholarship programme which enabled me to get into Cornell University in the first place.

Bob Smock was a short man with a soft determination to undermine apartheid in his own way. Every day, without fail, Uncle Bob would circle Day Hall, the administration building where President Frank Rhodes held office, with a placard saying 'Divest from South Africa'. I saw him there throughout the heat of summer and on any icy snow day in the winter. He did not need a crowd to convey his simple and powerful message. Divest. People walked around him, stared at him and largely seemed to ignore him over the years. But Uncle Bob showed up faithfully, a one-man conscience of Cornell on apartheid South Africa. On weekends, he would stop by our apartment and drop off a bag of juicy apples.

I learnt so much from Uncle Bob. One, that a professor on the other side of the world would give dedicated time to remind his university of the immorality of apartheid and its duty to divest from companies doing business in the country where it was a policy. Another lesson was something I treasure to this day – the important role of the individual as an activist. South African protests require crowds to invigorate the movement. Protestors, I noticed, do things in a crowd that they would never do on their own. But such herd instincts come at a cost – group think. Like Bob, I am congenitally unable to follow a crowd. The independence of the activist who thinks for him/herself still appeals to me. And then, of course, the fact that this was a white man who showed compassion and commitment to the struggle for freedom in black South Africa – that moved me greatly.

When Uncle Bob died in April 1986, South Africans filled the church in downtown Ithaca. To my utter surprise, he had instructed that someone read his letter from the dead. It was a series of jokes that left the mourners in stitches. It was, after all, Uncle Bob who wrote in anticipation that 'the only reward (*professor perfectus*) one can look forward to is to be flattened into a herbarium specimen and put on a shelf and never looked at again'.

His was a life well-lived. The famous professor who had studied the respiration rate of apples under controlled-atmosphere storage conditions had ceased to breathe. He had, however, left a powerful legacy of academic excellence and social activism. That was the lasting lesson from Uncle Bob – these two commitments need not be separate pursuits.

Being invited to a conference on 'Education after Apartheid' in Pittsburgh in the state of Pennsylvania was one such instance in which academic and political commitments were perfectly merged. It was the courageous South African Dennis Brutus who arranged the conference, where American activist scholars joined with South Africans to contemplate the future of South Africa through the presentation of research on the state of education in the homeland. Dennis had gone into exile and become a major force internationally in spearheading the sports boycott of apartheid South Africa. But he was also an academic with a keen eye on the question of our preparedness to 'take over' once the apartheid regime fell.

I had prepared a paper for a panel to which the respondent was Joel Samoff, a professor from Stanford University – where I would shortly be heading. All I remember from that panel discussion was the elegance and sharpness of the respondent's comments. I was mesmerised. Joel had read the paper, pointed out its strengths, delineated the weaknesses of the argument, and suggested a way forward for the revision of the paper. This was serious academic engagement and I remember being caught between slight hurt (he took my paper apart) and enormous elation (he thought it was good) as it dawned on me that this was how academics interact with each other.

I was on a sharp learning curve that day in Pittsburgh. Good academics can critically engage their colleagues on academic work and have a beer afterwards. In South Africa, academic criticism can make you lifelong enemies. Egos are fragile and a critical comment can be taken personally. South African academics, at the English universities especially, have been socialised into the false politeness of the British academy. I remember a visit to an academic conference in Bristol and hearing a professor say of his colleague's work, 'Professor X, I do not in the slightest mean to even begin to suggest that ...' and I almost fell of my chair laughing because X had actually spoken nonsense. How would you learn without the directness of your peers' criticism? For an aspiring academic with barely a Master's under his belt, the experience was tough for me, but Joel, it turned out, was a compassionate critic who would spend hours commenting and writing on your work in ways that readied you for publication.

It was also at this conference that I met one of the most decent academics you would find anywhere – a young South African professor in exile by the name of Mokubung Nkomo. He would become one of my most valued mentors for many years. I would send Mokubung drafts of essays or assignments or manuscripts for publication and he would plod through all those papers with great care and detailed comments. I was thriving in my closing days at Cornell and, though it was tough, I had the embrace and love of Grace and we were about to start a family.

In fact, what made my studies abroad much more durable is that I was not alone. We went overseas as a married couple, which meant that I had care, comfort and company especially during the two long winters at Cornell.

When our son, Mikhail, was born in New York in 1987, he brought untold happiness into the family circle and became the centre of our lives. There is nothing better than coming home from a long day in tough classes to the open arms of your family and the excited chatter of your little boy. Sara's birth four years later doubled our joy. She was born at Stanford and completed the family bond. I saw how single South African students struggled outside the country because they did not have that 'coming home' experience that kept your life as a student in vital balance.

The two years of study on the scenic campus of Cornell was ending far too soon. Even though I revelled in the belief of my academic teachers and fellow students, my life ambitions were still modest. To obtain a Master's degree was for me, at the time, an unexpected feat. I was now in full preparation to go back home and plough back into the community what I had learnt at Cornell. This was much more than I had expected to achieve and I checked on flights back home even before graduation. Then something unexpected happened.

George Posner taught me curriculum theory. I loved this field of study even more than science education. The idea that knowledge could be organised towards powerful learning purposes held my attention then and it still does now. George was an outstanding thinker about curricula as a technical set of concerns. He taught me how to do curriculum analysis in ways nobody had taught me before or since my time in Ithaca, New York. So when George called me to see him urgently, I thought it would be about curriculum matters.

'I have just been to DOGS,' he said, 'and she gave me permission to ask you to join our doctoral programme.' What? I was flattered and confused in equal measure – what on earth was DOGS? 'Oh, that's the Dean of the Graduate School,' he explained. 'You are one of the best students I have had in curriculum theory and I would like you to continue studies with us, fully paid.' I sat there, stunned. I mumbled that I was honoured but asked if could I get back to him with an answer. Of course, I wanted to take the generous offer – *but wait*, I thought, *if Cornell really thinks I can do a PhD, maybe I can apply elsewhere and see what happens.*

So I applied to Stanford, Harvard and my first choice: the University of Wisconsin–Madison. When you choose to do doctoral studies, you choose a professor before you select a university. Stanford had Martin Carnoy, the author of *Education as Cultural Imperialism* and this kind of focus fitted well with my growing political activism. Harvard had Noel McGinn, and his work on international education could expand my horizons beyond the very American-centred education that I had been exposed to until then.

But Michael Apple was at UW–Madison and had written the

most important critical text of the time: *Ideology and Curriculum*. This work spoke to a growing interest I was developing in the politics of knowledge. George had invited Michael to speak to our class at Cornell and I was mightily impressed by his critical instincts as a curriculum scholar. I could not forget his injunction to think about education relationally rather than on its own terms. In other words, Apple was teaching us how to 'see' education in relation to social, economic and political power. The curriculum did not emerge out of thin air; it was the product of powerful interests. Given the intense criticism of the apartheid curriculum back home, I thought this man would be an excellent supervisor of a doctoral thesis if I was accepted.

To my surprise, all three schools replied quite quickly with a positive response. There was just one problem. They all sent standard document attachments that required information on how I would pay for my studies. Until now, I had been on a fully paid scholarship that enabled me to study at Cornell. There was no way I could find money for four years of doctoral studies. I had to accept the Cornell offer, I thought.

There was another problem, though. Cornell had a very small education department housed in the 'Ag School' or the School of Agricultural and Life Sciences, as mentioned. It's a long story related to Cornell's history as a land grant institution, which meant that education, as one example, was closely linked to extension and development work in rural America – unlike the classical disciplines at Harvard and Yale. I knew the work of my small group of education professors at Cornell. I had read all their books and many of their published articles. I had been to their homes and participated in their research projects. What more could I possibly learn from them? It would also be great to get away from the long, harsh, snowy winters of Ithaca where I first experienced serious 'wind-chill' and thought it was the Second Coming; we were all going to die.

While I was mulling over the choices in front of me, the apartment phone rang. It was Martin Carnoy from Stanford. 'Listen,' he said, 'we really like your application and I am calling to offer you full funding for tuition and accommodation and you can earn a stipend by working part-time as a science education supervisor in the teacher education programme. We will fly you and your family to San Francisco as well. We would like you to do your PhD at Stanford.'

I was speechless – but we started packing for the West Coast. Friends offered humour as advice: *you can freeze in the east or quake in the west*. Little did I know that we were going to experience what Californians often speculate to be the 'big one' – a massive earthquake measuring 6.9 on the Richter scale which killed 67 people in October 1989.

But for now, there was a little tremor to deal with at Cornell. I had to tell George about the Stanford bid and that I would be declining the offer from Cornell. The disappointment was etched in his face but George understood and wished me well.

Something much more fundamental had changed inside of me. For the first time, I realised that I really could do well in my academics, and to do this at some of the best universities in the world was a massive boost to my confidence. The truth is that I was no different a person from the boy running after a soccer ball at school or the first-year dropout from university. What had changed was the messaging system that my professors, my fellow students and the whole system of graduate education was telling me: *you are smarter than you think*.

I was not alone. As I listened to the many South African students who came on this American-funded programme, the stories were similar. There was a friend who had failed chemistry at UWC but was now a PhD in chemistry from one of the top US universities and would return home as a professor of chemistry. In fact, on this funded programme, all but a few achieved their degrees and, unlike students from other African countries, almost all the South Africans returned home. Another friend was told by a white South African professor that he could not do engineering because 'blacks cannot think in three dimensions'. He would study in the US and of course, go on to become a professor of engineering.

'Look to your left and then look to your right,' another friend recalled from his time at a South African university. 'By the end of the term, one of you will be gone.' He was a white South African at a Pretoria university so I realised this deadening of expectations was standard fare across institutions. Now he was at MIT in Boston and when the professor said, 'Look to your left ...' he muttered, '*Hier gaan ons alweer.*' (Here we go again.) Except this time the professor said, 'The one on your left could become the next CEO of IBM and the person on your right, the CEO of another high-tech company.' Same student, different message.

South African academics with their British degrees resented

the American system of grading. I would sit through many cocktails and listen to criticism meant for my ears about the hyperinflation of the US grading system and the hyperbole contained in letters of reference. Heavily influenced by the Oxbridge culture with a particularly punitive view of student assessment, lecturers boasted about the 'standards' of university education at home and the rigours of evaluation. When I returned to teach and lead at South African universities, I quickly found that there was not much rigour to speak of in the former white institutions and that there was more than a little insecurity lurking in the criticism of American higher education.

But there was one more important insight I gained on my learning journey starting at Cornell. The top professors were mostly humble, accessible and nice people. They carried their fame lightly. Few of them paraded their accomplishments down the corridors of learning. This to me was curious. I had mainly seen arrogance and even remoteness in the attitudes of professors in class and on television, as in one of my favourite television series those days, *The Paper Chase*, dubbed into Afrikaans as *Beste Professor*.

It was not only the academics though. One lazy weekend, I was on campus waiting for a bus to take me to my Cornell apartment up the steep hill. I sat down next to an older man who was visiting for one of those very common US university events – the alumni reunion. After a brief chat (we were both spread out on the grass at the bus stop), he suddenly introduced himself. 'Oh, I'm Heimlich, Henry Heimlich,' he said.

'I'm Jonathan Jansen, from South Africa.' Wait. No. It can't be. So I sat up for a few seconds, wondering aloud: 'As in the Heimlich manoeuvre?' I asked him with some hesitation in my voice.

'That's me, yes.'

This sense of being human made a lasting impression on me. It even reflected in the clothes they wore. Kenneth Strike, my philosophy of education professor, wore the same pair of worn takkies for years. It looked terrible. None of the professors wore ties, except for special occasions. George was in jeans most of the time.

Most of all, they spoke like normal human beings rather than trying to impress you with big words. Even in their academic writings, most of the time the research was presented in digestible form for a broader audience rather than in the arcane language of specialisation of a particular field. That learning stuck with me to this day: that truly smart people can communicate on the other side of complexity. They would have worked through the difficult concepts or methods and could explain them simply and straightforwardly.

In other words, my very definition of what it meant to be smart was being transformed during those critical two years at Cornell. But what I was about to experience on the other coast of the US was going to challenge me to the point of giving up academic studies. Off to California.

You must show up

Of all the memories of teaching at school and university, one trio of students stands out in my memory. As the dean in the Faculty of Education at the University of Pretoria in the early 2000s, I decided to build a course-based doctoral programme, which was not allowed and certainly not funded in the South African higher education system. The dissertation-only route, an English university hangover, was still guarded as sacred in the elite universities.

And so, seven times a year, students from around the world would attend classes starting on Thursday evenings and ending on Saturday afternoons. The teaching slots ran from 4 pm to 8 pm on Thursday and Friday, and for the full day on Saturday with tough homework assignments for overnight completion. As with all education degrees, the students were mainly full-time working professionals, which suited the programme design since I could build their knowledge and experiences into the seven core modules that preceded the full dissertation requirement.

All students booked accommodation for the three days and two nights, except Itumeleng Molala, Dan More and Mamolahluwa Mokoena. What the trio did instead truly astounded me. Two of them were ranking officials in the department of education of the North West province, and the other was a junior academic at the University of the North West (formerly UNIBO or the University of Bophuthatswana). After the Thursday night class, which ended around 9.30 pm, they undertook the 317-kilometre trip home, in order to work during the day, and then made the same three-and-a-half-hour trip back to Pretoria the next day.

All three obtained their doctorates in the minimum time. Today, Itumeleng and Dan are senior officials in education and 'Mamo' is a professor and director of teaching and learning at North West University.

That was sacrifice. That was showing up.

* * *

When the plane landed in San Francisco in the autumn of 1987, I was met by the student president of the Stanford African Students Association (SASA) – a shining and smiling man from Senegal called Bakary Diame. He had been a doctoral student on 'The Farm' for years before I came and would continue to be for years after I left. 'The Farm' is the affectionate name for the campus named after Leland and Jane Stanford's son, Leland Junior, who died of typhoid fever at a young age and whose parents then turned over their beautiful farmlands for the establishment of this West Coast university in his memory.

Everything in California seemed different from our experiences on the East Coast and at Cornell in particular. People seemed friendlier – 'It must be the warmer weather,' someone offered. Where Ithaca was a rural campus about four hours' drive from Manhattan, Palo Alto was a sprawling city with great schools, scores of cafés and a mere 40-minute drive south of San Francisco during non-peak hours. This was before the explosion of technology companies across the city, the dot-com boom, as well as its collapse and recovery.

Neighbours came over to greet us in our student-family apartment and there were several welcoming ceremonies for new graduate students. Californians were incredibly warm and supportive but what happened with a neighbour, Dick, was truly unexpected. Dick took care of his young child while his wife studied for a PhD in English. He used to visit me regularly at night – always in shorts and barefooted – and asked lots of questions about apartheid, a monstrosity that intrigued this young Californian.

We became good friends and I shared with him the wonderful times we'd had at Cornell. I must have mentioned, in passing, that we were paying off a hefty hospital bill. We had discovered, belatedly, that we were underinsured for a caesarean birth in upstate New York. One night, Dick showed up and left a cheque for $10 000 (a huge amount of money, and a fortune in those days, especially for a student) on the coffee table. I immediately gave it back. Grace and I agreed that we could not accept this gift. This back-and-forth went on for some time and eventually we took the money and paid off the hospital bill. In the end, that gift gave massive relief to my young family.

Cornell was extremely hilly and required a campus bus to get up or down to classes. Stanford was flat and that enabled me to hire a bicycle to get to classes, the library, or sight-seeing on and around the campus. Enjoying my new environment, I also felt fairly confident with the commendations that came with a Cornell degree but my self-belief was about to be shattered.

The very first class I took was outside of the School of Education, in political science, where the professor was Charles Drekmeier. It was a small group of about 10 students and the reading assigned for discussion was Thomas Kuhn's stunning book *The Structure of Scientific Revolutions*. Eager to impress, I had read it from cover to cover, knowing that smart participation was key to success in these environments. After Drekmeier's introduction to the seminar, I jumped right in. That was my biggest mistake.

For the rest of the hour-and-a-half session, I was reduced to a spectator at a tennis match. Yes, I had read the book, but the other nine students had done more. They had read commentaries on the book and the author's response to some of his critics. They had synthesised Kuhn's arguments, but had also gone beyond that important elementary step to draw out the meanings of his use of 'paradigms' for disciplines beyond the physical sciences and examine his theory of how knowledge changes in comparison with other great thinkers in the philosophy of science. I was sitting in the middle of one side of the long table and my head turned constantly from side to side as the debate raged furiously among the other doctoral students.

I sat there in shock. This was a mistake. I might have graduated with a Master's but this was next level. By the time I reached Escondido Village, the apartment we had just moved into, I was seriously thinking of ending my studies right then and going home. Rather than make a complete fool of myself, and waste scholarship money, it was wise to bail out early. I sank onto the bed with a lump in my throat and tears in my eyes. This was the end of my learning journey. *There is no way I can keep up, let alone compete with these very smart students*, I thought.

Somewhere in the middle of that night, I had this discussion with myself. *You come from the Cape Flats. You have already overcome great hurdles to get this far. Every time you were knocked down, you got back up again. You can do this. You have survived tough things before. Get back in the ring.*

That kind of thing.

The next morning, I pulled myself together and made the decision: *I am going back in there but with one difference. I am now going to study harder and read more and debate tougher than these smart Stanford students.* That was the day I put my reading and study and sleeping habits into overdrive. *To compete in this environment*, I told myself, *you've got to show up.*

Years later, I would invite Oprah Winfrey to the University of the Free State, where I was Vice-Chancellor. During her memorable visit, I remember one of my students asking the great businesswoman how she had made it out of a miserable childhood and an early life of abuse. In typical style, Oprah was brief and to the point: 'When you get that one opportunity to impress, you show up.' I will never forget that wisdom.

Showing up at Stanford was definitely not easy. While Cornell was a serious Ivy League institution, Stanford was several notches up in academic intensity. Every student seemed super-smart – not only the professors. What was different from the East Coast, though, was that on the surface, everyone seemed very, well, Californian. That calm was deceptive, as one of the locals explained: 'We are like ducks. On the surface of the water, everything looks calm but underneath, the legs are paddling wildly.'

You could easily be fooled by the academic surface here. One day, we were waiting for the statistics professor to show up. He was late – something unusual for US academics. The mix of education and psychology students were talking among themselves when I noticed a barefooted man with wild hair come through the door at the back of the long classroom. He had a dirty T-shirt that read 'Psychotic State'. My heart went out to the poor soul. He must have walked onto this campus without any gates and got lost.

As the man approached the front of the class, I caught up with him and was about to lead him gently out of the room when he wrote his name and surname on the board. It was the stats prof. I turned around as smoothly as I could, pretending that I was simply returning to my seat for the start of class.

My assigned supervisor was a brilliant economist of education but when I first met him, sticking out of his backpack was a tennis racket. Martin Carnoy was easygoing in everything he did but that demeanour belied an incredible work ethic – and that was an early and significant learning for me on the Stanford campus. The top academics work really hard. I started to notice that he never left his office early, always punching away on his computer keyboard, working through yet another book. And I noticed that his secretary, Ellen, a gentle old lady, stayed late as well.

Martin became my role model for what it meant to show up. His academic pedigree was impressive. Among his teachers at the University of Chicago had been the Nobel economists Theodore Schultz, who gave us human capital theory, and the conservative scholar Milton Friedman. Here's the strange thing: as conservative as Friedman might have been, Martin Carnoy had become a radical professor who supported left-wing movements in Latin America, decried American imperialism abroad, and in later life wrote a book in praise of the Cuban education system.

With his progressive leanings, Martin was an exceptionally competent economist of education who taught his subject well. His calm and casual demeanour could sometimes be infuriating. For example, he was never on time for his student supervision appointments and one day I made it clear to him that his lateness was unacceptable. He made the excuse that 'when you go to the doctor, you wait'. I could see him smiling even as he drew this ridiculous analogy.

What he did teach me was not to take yourself too seriously, to stick to the facts, and never to go into development work without first acquainting yourself with the context of your proposed actions. That latter learning was something that, to this day, I take very seriously – know your context first before you jump in with proposals and ideas.

And yet context was exactly what I struggled with in the specific programme that I was enrolled in at Stanford. Whereas Cornell allowed you to study a broad range of courses and still get your degree, Stanford's programme in international development education (IDE, which was a programme under SIDEC, the Stanford International Development Committee) required that all doctoral students take a set menu of courses, which offered social science perspectives on education. So, for example, you had to take courses on the economics of education, the anthropology of education, the sociology of education and the politics of education. There was just one problem. The professors teaching those courses were disciplinarians – in other words, economists, anthropologists, sociologists and political scientists. None of them were classroom teachers like myself.

In every class, I complained. You cannot reduce the complex acts of teaching and learning to social structures in sociology, or production functions in economics. Nor was every transaction in the science classroom a reflection of the politics of the state. I could not see how another reading on 'culture among the Inuit' could possibly relate to the organisational cultures of schooling in deprived communities. And the sociology of the spread of mass education was interesting but had little to do with the social organisation of schooling in apartheid South Africa. I was frustrated but made the case in the seminars for taking teachers and students seriously as real actors within the drama of education and not simply as unthinking, reflexive tools of an oppressive state.

To their credit, my professors heard me out, even though every now and again there would be a harsh exchange on their 'structuralist' account of schooling and my more 'agential' view of teachers. Then something happened that I did not expect. Martin had married again and his second wife was a school teacher. One day, he pulled me aside and said something like this: 'You know, you were right. I was wrong. There is a lot more happening inside classrooms than I thought.'

But I had changed too. I knew my strengths: the ability to do close-up analyses of within-school and classroom events, while simultaneously being able to hold a social lens over those myriad transactions that constitute teaching, learning, assessment and curriculum. I had the best of both worlds but still not enough of the former. I simply did not have enough theory and research on school- and classroom-based studies, especially when undertaken from a critical perspective. So I made up my own curriculum, so to speak.

Bruce King was a kindred spirit. He was doing all those teaching and learning courses in a different School of Education programme with great scholars like Lee Shulman, Myron Atkin and Decker Walker. Our paths crossed and a deep friendship began. If I was frustrated by the distant social science perspective on education, he was unhappy with the lack of critical perspectives on what happens inside schools and classrooms. What could we do?

We designed our own curriculum called 'Critical Perspectives on Classroom Research'. Next, we approached the dean for funding a series of visiting professors from other universities, since Stanford did not have scholars concerned with critical theories of education. We were ambitious, calling on the likes of the prolific Henry Giroux from Boston University who authored one of my favourite texts of the time, *Theory and Resistance in Education* (and who brought along Peter McLaren); and Patti Lather from Ohio State University whose well-cited piece 'Research as Praxis' was ground-breaking for its times. These were among the 'who's who' in critical theories of education at the time. Most of the speakers came without requesting honoraria – an invitation to Stanford carried its own currency.

We attracted good audiences for the various lunch-time talks and the debates were intense and invigorating. In the process, something remarkable happened: when the university did not offer what we wanted in the curriculum, we created our own learning experience as students.

One day, I could not find Bruce. He did not show up for a meeting, which was most unusual. We needed to plan a joint paper but he was nowhere to be found. Eventually, I found a number for my trusted collaborator and I was put through to him. Bruce spoke in short sentences. I am sorry for not being in touch. I would like to see you. Can you come to the hospital?

Hospital? Bruce, what is wrong? You could have told me. And so on. I rushed to the hospital in San Francisco and there he was, looking even more lean than normal. What's wrong, buddy?

Then in rapid succession: I have Aids, Jonathan. I am dying. I am gay.

It is hard to explain how those three messages hit me. I wanted to hug him and tell him it was okay. I wanted to apologise for my conservative, evangelical upbringing that condemned gay people out of hand. I wanted to give him hope and imagine I had not heard what he said and tell him about the next series of speakers for our self-made curriculum. But I stood there, stunned, holding his hand and telling Bruce what an amazing person he was.

Shortly afterwards, Bruce died. It was a time of immense sadness and I struggled to get through my speech at his memorial. By that time, I had long overcome the backward attitudes of my upbringing with respect to gay people. I had simply met too many decent, outstanding and often devout Christians who were gay and lesbian to hold on to the hurtful bigotry of my socialisation. If there were any lingering traces of doubt, my friendship with Bruce washed them away. How could I judge a man differently, a man who became a best friend at Stanford, simply because I now discovered that he was gay? That was sheer madness. And yet the stigma and fear of rejection were real for people like Bruce, even in the gay-friendly Bay Area where I was now living. Why else would he have held this important part of his identity secret from many of his friends on campus? With Bruce's passing, I had reached yet another important landmark in my life and learning: that the bonds of friendship can and should cancel out the bigotries that we all carry within us.

I was never alone in my academic pursuits. Over four years at Stanford, I was blessed with many friends who aided my learning journey. Dan Perlstein was another close friend. He too was a critical scholar doing his doctorate with a very accomplished historian David Tyack, whose famous book, *The One Best System*, had become a classic in the history of American education. As a budding historian, Dan's work was on the Freedom Schools of the Student Non-Violent Co-ordinating Committee (SNCC, or 'Snick' by sound), a principal channel of youthful commitment in the American Civil Rights Movement. The bearded and long-haired Dan, a quintessential Californian, had none of the subtleties of Bruce King, as I was about to discover in a most unpleasant way.

Our bond was again a shared sense of 'the critical' when it came to any deep understanding and analysis of education. So we decided to share draft papers before sending them out for publication. I had a rough draft on People's Education and he gave me something about the Freedom Schools. Perhaps we could even do a comparative study, we thought. A week or more later, we got together to share our comments on each other's papers. 'This,' said Dan, 'is the biggest load of crap I have ever read.' That's how Dan gives it to you and unless you've known him for a long time, his comments can sting. He had scribbled all over my now-crumpled paper. I am not sure I completely hid my hurt but I mumbled something like, 'Why do you say that?'

It was the best commentary I could have received. My writing was pretentious and indirect. Political commitment stood in for critical analysis. There was little theory to take the argument 'beyond the case' and even less data, other than endless personal anecdotes. Dan was right. It took me a few days to recover and then I rewrote the article and gave it right back to him.

Ours is a friendship that endures to this day with Dan working as professor of history at the University of California at Berkeley. I learnt from the still-bearded Dan that a real friend will tell you the truth when it comes to your academic writing. It helped me a lot then and continues to be the way in which I communicate as a critical friend on the works of my colleagues and students.

After a year at Stanford, I was passing comfortably. But there was much more to learn. I was again in sponge mode, absorbing every learning opportunity. Then, Bakary, the senior student who had collected me from the airport, came to see me with a determined expression on his face. 'We think you would be the ideal person to take over from me as president of the Stanford African Student Association. The international cause of the day, the struggle against apartheid, would give SASA leverage on campus and in the Bay Area community.' So I took on the presidency of SASA.

One of the most valuable learnings that came from being in a programme concerned with international development education (IDE) was that I was taught the skill of thinking comparatively. This would prove invaluable in the analysis of education. It prevented narrow thinking about education problems and the kind of exceptionalism that threatens scholarship in countries like South Africa. Being taught to think as a comparativist also helped my growing identity as an internationalist. I refused then, and now, to limit my intellectual pursuits or my social commitments to a narrow sense of what it means to be a

South Africanist.

'Comrade,' asked the petrol attendant at an Umtata station shortly after I arrived back from California in 1991, 'what are you?'

I knew what was coming. 'Well, I'm Catholic.'

'No, no, Comrade, you know what I mean: what are you really?'

'Okay,' I said, 'the game is up. I confess. I'm gay.'

'Comrade! No. Where are you from?'

'I am from everywhere,' I told the now clearly frustrated petrol man. This so often happened to me – he wanted to place me into one of four racial boxes of apartheid – white, Indian, coloured or African. By nailing me down to one identity, he could then proceed with the conversation.

The question of identity still informs my politics. I was born in the beautiful rural Boland town of Montagu. But my parents moved quickly to Port Elizabeth in search of work before settling in Cape Town, where I grew up. But I feel as close to Harare as I do to San Francisco or Cape Town and, in later years, to Durban, Pretoria and Bloemfontein, where our children grew up and enjoyed their schooling.

Where are you from? For me, this is not only a question of geography but one of history, sociology and politics – it is a question about my deepest commitments. For that reason, I have struggled to sing the national anthem and I fight every time the South African government threatens to introduce some kind of oath of allegiance in schools (normally when there is a crisis in governance), for that kind of narrowmindedness carries within it the seeds of xenophobia, always eager to sprout under conditions of nationalist fervour.

This understanding of my place in the world shaped my understanding of the scope of my commitments as president of SASA at Stanford. As an internationalist, I believed that a pan-African approach was worth pursuing, beyond the pressing issue of apartheid and South Africa.

At that time, there were constant news reports about the famine in the Sudan. So we pulled together activists from on- and off-campus, and loaded a plane with food and medical supplies which flew from San Francisco airport all the way to Sudan. The north/south battles in Sudan made for some delays as our political and logistics teams tried to figure out how to ensure the goods got to the people. I remember going to the airport with a small group of activists and being amazed that, as students, we could pull off something of this magnitude.

Leading SASA was not all plain sailing. The Nigerian students at Stanford (as at Cornell) thought of themselves as a special breed of Africans and, despite hours of meetings to dissuade them, they insisted on having their own African student organisation. It was also the most tribalist African student group at both Cornell and Stanford. One way this sentiment reached me was through the suspicion that I was not really African. Africans did not have surnames like Jansen, which sounded like a white, Dutch surname. I had little time for such backwardness.

Another group with whom SASA could never really partner on major projects was the organisation for African-American students. There was definitely some resentment about what they saw as the generous American funding of Africans from the continent while their people did not enjoy the same levels of financial support from their own government, foundations or corporations. I understood those concerns but I also could not grasp why working together would not help all of us.

But SASA pushed ahead and the next big project after the Sudan airlift was to bring to the campus some of the leaders in the southern African region at a time when it really did seem as if the apartheid regime was on its last legs. First, I decided to bring Graça Machel to campus shortly after her husband, Samora Machel, was killed in an air crash. As students, we believed he was assassinated by the apartheid regime. Graça was then quite shy and reserved, not the feisty widow of Nelson Mandela who would go on to serve as chancellor of the University of Cape Town. On campus, she needed a Portuguese interpreter, but that made little difference to the warm but firm heart of Samora's successor in the struggle for freedom, as we saw it.

That event was followed by a disaster.

We were on the eve of Namibia's liberation in 1990. It was about this time that a South African occupation force killed more than 100 South West Africa People's Organisation (SWAPO) soldiers. I can remember the deep outrage at this atrocity and decided that one way to respond was to bring SWAPO's representative at the United Nations, Helmut Angula, into a campus dialogue with Chester Crocker, the man whom President Reagan had appointed as Assistant Secretary of State for African Affairs. Crocker had a daughter studying at

Stanford so it was not too difficult getting him to come to the West Coast.

The story goes that Crocker attracted the attention of the Reagan administration for a paper he had written in the journal *Foreign Affairs* on constructive engagement, a policy position that basically advocated for talking with the white regime to resolve the apartheid question, rather than a more confrontational stance. As activist students, we found the policy reprehensible, of course. Nonetheless, SASA invited the two men to kick off our annual Africa Day event in 1990.

To my mind, this was an opportunity for Angula to dress down Crocker by showing him the consequences of constructive engagement – the mass killing of SWAPO soldiers on the eve of independence. The problem is that Angula was soft-spoken, reticent and without even a hint of distress at what had just happened in southern Africa. Crocker, on the other hand, was assertive, confident and could think on his feet as we peppered him with questions from the floor. The man from Washington ran rings around our hero and I had some questions to answer from the Africanists on campus.

Here, too, there was a valuable lesson that stays with me to this day. *Showing up entails taking risks.* Most times it works but any ambition comes with the risk of failure. That is no reason not to take risks.

I have learnt how to budget for disappointment and how to learn from failure. Somehow, when you prepare for the possibility of things not working out, you are better able to handle a negative result. On the other hand, the payoff to risk-taking is huge, since in my experience, you have a hit rate of about 80 per cent success, and that works for me. As a result, I am not one to sink into depression because something failed and certainly not one to avoid risking a great idea simply because it might not work out.

There is one danger I was always aware of and that is that *you cannot show up for everything.* At a place like Stanford, there were literally scores of activist and academic projects that I could join. Almost every lunch-hour, there was a famous speaker on any number of interesting topics, the pamphlet nailed to a tree or pasted onto a bulletin board somewhere. It was a veritable treat for a hungry graduate student. But I had to choose.

I chose not to become active in Our Developing World, an amazing overseas study group that took Bay Area communities to trouble spots in the world, including South Africa. The couple running this programme, Vic and Barby Ulmer, showed up at every South African event on the Stanford Campus and once took my family for a weekend camp in the beautiful Yosemite National Park. It was tempting to become involved in the anti-apartheid movement in the Bay Area, which was very strong in places like Berkeley thanks to powerful activists like Congressman Ron Dellums and, of course, the black churches in cities like Oakland, where cleric Allan Boesak was a favourite speaker. Dockworkers in San Francisco were stalwarts in the struggle and refused to offload ships carrying cargo from South Africa. It was tempting to join these groups but I decided on a more measured approach by using the campus as a springboard for our activism. And it was here, on campus, where I was about to learn a lifelong lesson in solidarity.

To some extent, I had cover as a black South African student. The general approach from the university authorities was one of understanding, if not support. Despite marches and petitions, the Board of Trustees really dug in their heels on divestment. But the approach to American students was much more ruthless. It started with a sit-in by mainly undergraduate students at the president's office.

The student sit-in was to press the university to divest its stocks from American companies doing business in apartheid South Africa. Stanford was a wealthy private university with little of the tradition of protests in the large publics, like the University of California campuses such as UCLA and UC-Berkeley. The next thing I knew was that there were helicopters overhead and heavy-handed police dragging the students from the corridors of the president's office. I was horrified. Was this American democracy? Worse was to follow. Those brave students were not allowed to study at Stanford University again. My heart was broken but my resolve deepened. This fight must continue. In the process, I learnt so much about how young white and black students would sacrifice their studies and jeopardise their careers for a struggle thousands of miles away.

And sometimes, one of them would die for the cause. In my desire to learn more about South Africa and indeed the continent, rather than drawing on experience alone, I signed up for a class by Professor Joel Samoff, who at that time was part of the IDE programme in the School of Education. The course itself was an introduction to Africa, examining the pre-colonial, colonial and independence periods. I found this course fascinating, not only because the content was new, but because Joel Samoff was probably one of the best undergraduate teachers I had met. Joel's preparation was thorough and his readings extensive, but what really marked this course as special were the intellectual demands that he made on students through engagement in class and the assignments. I lapped it up.

In that class sat a young and small-built blonde undergraduate student. She was quiet and passed as simply another Stanford student. I did not speak to any of the students because I was a graduate student who had sneaked into a class not really tailored for older students.

The next thing I heard about her, about five years later, was that the young student was dead. Her car was ambushed in Gugulethu township in Cape Town during a volatile march of some PAC students. She had inserted herself into the struggle and worked in gender and development with other women activists in the black community. But the protestors did not know that the white woman in the car was on their side. Amy Biehl died a horribly tragic death. Years later, a fellow Stanford student and friend, Steve Gish, would write a full-length biography in Amy's honour: *Amy Biehl's Last Home: A bright life, a tragic death, and a journey of reconciliation in South Africa*. That subtitle reflected her dedication. I was learning, once again, what sacrificial living really was about when it came to commitment to a cause – Amy showed up with her life.

LESSON 4

Make things happen when they do not

Lesego Suping was a small but commanding presence wherever she went. Born with osteogenesis imperfecta or brittle bone disease, her small body was permanently confined to a wheelchair. Simple tasks became impossible, even life-threatening. But you never noticed the wheelchair or any sign of brittleness – only her immaculate grooming and infectious smile. 'Good morning, Prof! How are you today?'

I would come to learn that her natural warmth and generosity belied a steely determination to make things happen. But this new request made no sense. The tiny black woman had rolled into the open space outside my office with two huge white dudes, one on each side of her wheelchair, like bodyguards of sorts. *What now?*

'Prof,' Lesego had started, towering in confidence over the two muscular men in their own chairs. 'We want you to give us space in the Callie for wheelchair rugby.' The Callie was the massive university auditorium used for everything from graduations to netball tournaments.

I dared not share the oxymoron that sprang to mind. Wheelchairs and rugby? I allowed for the private thought: *rugby lands people in wheelchairs!* More practically, this was a difficult one because the Callie was *always* overbooked for events of all kinds, including mega-church services. Lesego wasn't smiling any more as she trained those fierce brown eyes on her rector. She knew that almost every speech I made contained a commitment to serving our staff and students with disabilities. Of course, Lesego. Somebody was going to have to give up space in the Callie.

When I read on Facebook early in 2019 that Lesego had passed away 'after struggling with some health issues', I was heartbroken. Somebody posted a picture of Lesego on campus, at the spot where a new ramp had been installed for wheelchairs.

She made things happen.

* * *

Myron 'Mike' Atkin was a gentle soul. Before I arrived at Stanford, he had served a spell as dean of the university's School of Education. He was also a kindred spirit, someone who had written some very interesting pieces on science education in the classroom. Naturally, I was drawn to Mike and enrolled in one of his classes outside of the prescribed courses of my programme. It was a treat. Mike's delivery was sophisticated and his sense of the history of science education was mesmerising. It was also such a relief to be in a class with an expert who understood the complexities as well as the entrancement of studying teaching and learning in real classrooms.

There was only one problem. There were no critical perspectives on teaching and learning, whether from feminist or antiracist or class analyses of education. As our friendship developed, I summoned the courage to point this out to the former dean. His reaction caught me off-guard: 'Okay, so why don't you teach what's missing?' *Yikes. What?*

So I designed a course called 'Controversies in the Classroom' with Mike as the faculty sponsor for the new class. The course was given one or two credits and I proceeded to pull together some critical readings and design the overall curriculum. We advertised and about 10 students showed up, including two South Africans, a fair number for a graduate student class. Mike sat in on some of those classes and I was nervous at first. I'd never thought I would be tasked to teach a course at Stanford University of all places. But it went well and Mike's support was invaluable.

Later, I would sometimes meet South African students on campus who were well-known activists in education and development back home. They would complain that the curriculum did not fully meet their expectations. I could never understand this. You are surrounded by the best libraries in the world with access to leading experts in their fields and you complain that the course does not offer you what you want? Create your own education, I would advise. Make things happen.

Still, I was restless. Activism for me always meant more than marching and singing, let alone burning and breaking. I wanted to channel my activism through the one thing I could do and that was teaching. Around that time, the university offered alternative education opportunities for students to become involved in. One such programme was called SWOPSI – the Stanford Workshops on Political and Social Issues. I signed up and proposed a course on South African education and politics. To my surprise, the course was accepted by the authorities and about 25 students showed up.

All these extracurricular involvements happened even as I was doing my regular courses and preparing for the proposal defence in the School of Education. American universities require about two years of coursework followed by a thesis proposal, which upon defending successfully, certifies you to go 'into the field' for data collection. You then return to the university to 'write up' the thesis and then defend it before a full panel of experts who decide whether you get the degree or not. By the time you defend your thesis, however, it is understood that you are ready to defend and pass. I do not know of any students who fail at this stage because it would be a terrible reflection on the supervisor if this did happen.

The British institutions, whose ideas still regulate educational arrangements in former colonies like South Africa, do not have any coursework arrangements for a doctorate. To this day, I cannot understand how it is possible to train a PhD student without a solid base of coursework offered by experts in a range of allied fields, to broaden and deepen the education of the doctoral candidate. But South African academics are steeped in colonial tradition without knowing it and so I found it difficult to convince colleagues differently on my return home – but I did it anyway.

Martin Carnoy, my supervisor, wanted me to get my PhD over and done with: 'Why don't you go into East Palo Alto, collect your data, and write up the PhD?' At the time, East Palo Alto was the poor version of Palo Alto, an economically depressed community of mainly African-American and Latino families. I visited schools there and once or twice, went to church in that community. It was hard to believe that just over the bridge crossing Highway 101, you could have such an affluent community (Palo Alto) co-existing with such an impoverished neighbourhood (East Palo Alto). Today, East Palo Alto has become gentrified in parts because of the explosion of Silicon Valley.

While I could see parallels in underdevelopment between East Paly and South Africa, my heart was set on Zimbabwe, which achieved independence in 1980. Now, almost 10 years later, many education activists thought that a new South Africa would be able to learn from the Zimbabwean experiment with radical education. The signs were all positive. In the years following the collapse of Ian Smith's white-minority regime, Zimbabwe under Robert Mugabe had some amazing achievements to celebrate: Near universal access to primary education; and experiments in mass education, such as education with production (borrowed from an exiled South African entrepreneur in next-door Botswana), Zimbabwe Science (ZIMSCI brought science 'practicals' to poor areas) and ZINTEC, the integrated national teacher education course (mass-producing teachers for the expanded school system). I was enthralled. Most of all, Zimbabwe had centralised the development of new syllabi in a powerful curriculum development unit led by a fighter from the war, the venerable Fay Chung. I simply had to go there and extract 'lessons' for a post-apartheid South Africa.

There was only one small issue. It was very difficult to gain access to Zimbabwe, which was experiencing post-war insurgencies and conflicts, mainly from apartheid South Africa. Zimbabwe's political establishment was highly suspicious of researchers claiming to come and do studies of various kinds but who were in reality spies for apartheid South Africa or imperialist America (in the language of those days). The fact that I was a South African called Jansen probably did not help my case.

A fellow student in my programme, Laura Gibney, had to wait more than two years before obtaining permission and I knew that this would be impossible for me. I needed to finish this degree, get back home and make a difference. I had no intention of sitting in California for two or more years waiting to go to Zimbabwe. I applied and waited but then decided to make a plan.

Soon afterwards, I was asked by Creative Associates International (a USAID-funded minority contractor) in Washington DC to join a team doing a sector analysis of education in Zimbabwe. Would I serve as the curriculum expert? Of course, I said yes. This was my opportunity to go to Zimbabwe and do my data collection during and beyond the term of the assignment.

On arrival in the first African country that I had visited outside of South Africa, I was ecstatic. The problem is, I had no experience in consulting and I was with a crack team of highly experienced management consultants, one of whom was our team leader, Dick Fehnel. I was about to learn hard skills through a harsh immersion experience.

One morning, Dick asked each of the team members (the economist, the teacher education specialist and others) to write up a mid-visit report on what we had found so far. I wrote my page and shared it with the group. 'This is useless,' said Dick. 'You cannot write in the flowery prose of an academic. You need to write as a consultant. What is the problem? How did you analyse it? What did you find? And what do you recommend? Rewrite please.'

It was a massive slap-down in front of the other team members. I was the Stanford guy so I could sense the pressure was on. I resented the way Dick taught me at the time. This experienced consultant from Oregon had a matter-of-fact way about him that rendered the man aloof but determined. Even his jokes carried a measure of terror for a beginner consultant, like this one: 'When you're up to your ass in alligators, it's hard to remember the original goal was to drain the swamp.' Ha, ha, ha but *gulp*. The reference was to the chaotic management of the education system as Zimbabwe fought Aids, historical backlogs and a suspected South African insurgency. In the meantime, I had to learn to write as a consultant.

It was a valuable lesson. Writing as a scholar is indeed different from writing as a consultant or writing as a columnist for a newspaper, as I would later find out. Writing as a consultant forces you to think technically and to write precisely. In later years, I thanked Dick, when he moved to South Africa with his wife Doreen to work until his retirement, for teaching me how to think and write as a consultant. It would help me make a decent living in subsequent years.

My first visit to Zimbabwe in 1989 was something of a reconnaissance trip. I got to know the senior people in politics and in the bureaucracy. I visited rural schools and communities across the country. I collected nearly every major policy and planning document concerned with curriculum. Once I got back to the States, I started to plan my return trip with or without the research visa I was still waiting on. I now knew something about the context; I had a rich network of people in and outside the capital Harare, and I had friends there who would put me up and help me save on accommodation costs. I finalised my research protocols and set off for Zimbabwe again in 1990 – on a tourist visa, rather than a research visa. I did not have official permission, but I had to make things happen or remain stuck in California.

The second visit was both easier and more difficult. On the one hand, I got access to senior politicians because they knew me from my previous visit, but I sensed something was not right. I asked for key curriculum documents not received on the earlier visit. But nobody gave them to me as I walked up and down the many floors of the head offices of the education ministry.

Then, one day, somebody gave me a bunch of materials that contained correspondence I should not have seen. Originating in the minister's office, the letter starting at the top of government said 'give him the documents'. But as the same document

75

travelled from top to bottom, each official added a comment: 'No, do not give it. We don't know who he is and how it could be used.' Then another: 'This information [the O- and A-level examination papers] is already in the public domain; give it to him,' only to find another instruction, even lower down, not to part with the documents. So I walked across the road and bought the necessary texts and old exam papers from a bookshop in Harare.

What I learnt that day was how fear and anxiety could entrap a bureaucracy while the apartheid government still operated across the border. But I also gained first-hand insight into bureaucratic pettiness and how it could weigh down efficiency if officials were not paying attention.

Still, I was enjoying my time in this newly liberated country. It is quite something as a black South African to feel completely free on your own continent. Comrades were everywhere. A well-known economist and activist once invited me to his home for dinner with other South Africans. He wanted me to meet a student called Botha. No, I said firmly, I have had enough of the Bothas back home. Apparently, the student also had no appetite for a Jansen from home. I missed the opportunity to meet a hero from South Africa called Thozamile Botha. Awkward. He, too, was fascinated with what this country north of the Limpopo could teach us after our liberation.

The foundation of my learning about curriculum policy was in fact being laid in this small and promising education experiment called Zimbabwe. The government had presented itself as the face of radical education reform based on Marxist-Leninist principles. This would be perfectly reflected in a new curriculum policy called the Political Economy of Zimbabwe (PEZ). I asked around for a copy of the PEZ. Nobody seemed to have it but my luck was about to change.

In the dead of night, a lecturer at the University of Zimbabwe (UZ) gave me the curriculum in a sealed brown envelope. I had to make sure nobody else ever saw this hot document or know that he had given it to me. It was, at the time, a mystery why a good thing like the new radical curriculum was being treated with such secrecy.

Late that night, I opened the envelope and read the document, which was about 10 pages long. It certainly was radical – outlining the social-science content of revolutionary ideas for teaching and learning and assessment. I was still puzzled, though, by the near-classified status of the document.

It did not take too many interviews with teachers, parents, officials and academics at UZ to find out why the government was petrified about its own radical schemes. Zimbabwe had one of the strongest school systems in the region. It had established a reputation for academic excellence built on that most venerated of colonial vestiges, the Cambridge O- and A-level examinations operated by the Cambridge Examination Syndicate. In science and mathematics, no country in the SADC region could match the students of former Rhodesia. If, in this most traditional and colonial of school systems, the government was going to introduce PEZ, there could be a national uprising that would destabilise its proud education system. Well, PEZ would never leave the safe in the ministry, where it was safely tucked away.

It was a powerful lesson to a young doctoral student concerned with curriculum policy for a future Azania, as some of us dared rename our country, even before its liberation from apartheid. While radical policies had an important symbolic value in rallying support for a nationalist cause, in this case, there was something much more difficult to deal with and that was what the reality on the ground would allow. It became the insight that informed my criticism of Outcomes Based Education (OBE) in South Africa in the pamphlet 'Ten reasons why OBE will fail' in 1998. And it is the same line of reasoning that informs my thesis that *decolonising the curriculum* will have very little impact on the organisation and purposes of knowledge in South African universities.

After another two or three visits to Zimbabwe without a government-issued research visa, I had enough data to write my dissertation. But I was restless. On a four-year scholarship, I had already finished the dissertation and there was still lots of time left. I needed to think about an academic job back home since it was now clear to me that being a teacher at one school was too limited a scope for what I could possibly do next – influence thousands of teacher trainees to make a difference in the nation's schools. So I did two things: talk to people and publish research.

The 'talking to people' at home did not go too well. An established professor from a Cape Town university came to the Bay Area and asked to meet with me. We provided him with a fancy meal with my student stipend and then, towards the end of the evening, I told him of my plans to return home. Was there any chance of a position at his university in comparative and international education? I did not expect his emphatic answer: 'No – over my dead body.' He did not explain why. Was I a threat? What could possibly be the reason for such an unkind response? He could have given me any number of off-ramps into unemployment but 'over my dead body'? I did not understand and started to feel sorry that I had made the investment in a sumptuous dinner.

A few weeks later, he dropped dead. The dean of his university called with a job offer. Seriously. Over his dead body.

A completed dissertation was not enough to satisfy my intellectual curiosity and I had some months to play with. Very few students finished a doctorate at Stanford within four years, yet I felt the need to do more. I published my research in some fancy journals and soon had a handful of good articles to list on my curriculum vitae. More could be done, though.

At about this time, I came under the very positive influence of one of my outstanding professors, a German-American called Hans Weiler. Hans came to America with enviable experiences that included exposure to the founders of the Frankfurt School of Critical Theory, including Theodor Adorno and a younger Jürgen Habermas. His discipline was political science, which he applied in the study of the state and legitimacy in education. Hans embedded within me an abiding interest in the politics of knowledge, which to this day, frames my work in curriculum theory – starting with my very first book project.

So I wrote to about 20 South Africans in different disciplines, from urban planning to dentistry, nursing, sociology, anthropology and the management sciences. I wanted them to think deeply about how race, power and politics are expressed within the content and constitution of their disciplines. It was an ambitious idea to ask mainly young scholars who were outstanding professionals in their craft to think about the politics of knowledge. Soon, the draft papers started trickling in and I learnt quickly that it is much more difficult producing an edited book than writing a single-authored monograph. Back and forth went the comments for revision. I read all the chapter drafts until I could thread them together in line with the theme of the politics of knowledge.

By the time I boarded the plane back home, the dissertation was done, the book (titled *Knowledge and Power*) was in production and about a dozen articles had appeared in scholarly and professional journals, mainly in the USA. My mother, who never talked to me about my academic work, made a short comment: 'I can see you did not waste your time in America.' It was her way of saying, *you made things happen over there*.

Back in California, while I was still mulling over the possibility of following up on the expression of interest at my dead visitor's university in Cape Town, the University of Durban-Westville (UDW) announced that it was looking for a Chair of Curriculum Studies. Somebody told me about this juicy job and I applied.

The interview was one of the strangest I had ever experienced. It took place at 3 am in California and so I had to make arrangements with the Center for African Studies to access their building and the office telephone at that awkward time.

Professor Jairam Reddy, the vice-chancellor, chaired the meeting with a number of the education academics in attendance. This was long before Skype or WhatsApp video so I found it difficult to engage without seeing people and their expressions. That was not necessary, though. After a few softball questions, the chairman asked me, 'When can you start?' I was stunned. And just like that, I got my first full professorship post in my first-ever academic appointment.

A few months later, in June 1991, I headed back to South Africa and after a brief stint working with education NGOs, I took up the position of Chair of Curriculum Studies at UDW in 1992.

I am not sure this had ever been done before – taking a new PhD and making him or her a full professor. I would never have done that and I am sure there were ripples around the campus about this unusual appointment. What made the difference, I think, is that by the time I got my PhD, I had also made a lot more things happen than the dissertation only.

This is the one other thing I learnt about the American academy. If you show signs of life as a graduate student, the professors take you very seriously. In other words, if you make things happen, then they make things happen for you. The opposite is sadly true as well. If you drag your feet as a student, everybody ignores you. You have to stand out, do more and do well. As the father of immunology Louis Pasteur once said, 'Chance favours the prepared mind.'

That is probably why the next invitation happened, something that would challenge my intellectual depth and my personal confidence. While I was still at Stanford in 1990, Martin Carnoy called me to ask if I would teach on a well-funded World Bank programme that trained senior civil servants from Malaysia in advances in education policy and planning. I was intimidated by the challenge, to be sure, but also excited to meet these colleagues from a country where my maternal line of ancestors came from as Malay slaves. My grandmother, for example, was named Kulsum, though everyone called her Katie, and she had roots in South East Asia.

I spent weeks preparing to teach these experienced education bureaucrats twice my age about the most recent advances in research on curriculum policy and planning in developing countries. It went well and we had some of the Malaysian colleagues over to our small student apartment for dinner. In the course of the evening, I realised that we used similar-sounding words back in Cape Town like *barakat* and *tramakassie*. 'We are cousins,' I joked with the visitors.

That experience not only put some money in my lean student bank account; it gave me the confidence that I could do advanced training in education policy, given the chance. My supervisor had made things happen for me, as did others.

'I would like you to present on a panel at CIES with me,' said my other professor, Hans Weiler. The Comparative and International Education Society has an annual conference and that year it would be hosted by Harvard University on the other side of the country. Hans was known to the students as a firm man and a fastidious scholar. He took his work detail very seriously. Where Martin might be an hour late for his student appointments, Hans was there before you. And so being asked by this outstanding academician to share a panel with him at a prestigious conference was certainly a challenge and an honour.

One of my papers for his classes dealt with the state and legitimacy in education in Zimbabwe and this thought piece caught his eye. Our panel proposal was accepted and so off to Harvard we went. Our slot was the graveyard session: early on a Sunday morning. There were fewer than 10 people present but we soldiered on. I did not think my paper was earth-shattering but something else was: that Hans Weiler thought I had something to say with him on an international stage. It is something I never forgot.

Years later, and with Hans now professor emeritus, I asked him whether he would join me one more time on a panel at CIES, at its 2019 Annual Conference, in San Francisco. It was a reunion I cherished. This time I could make something happen for my retired professor.

Set high standards

In all my years working with schools, I had not heard of a student in a poor rural school asking to take on additional subjects. The request made no sense. None of the disadvantaged schools have the teachers to do 'extra' subjects and many cannot even teach their fixed subjects well enough. Those students who do nine or 10 subjects, rather than the standard six or seven, are always from the elite high schools in the country. But Lindokuhle was a driven young man from Amangwane High School in rural KwaZulu-Natal with high standards for his school education and an early commitment to become a neurosurgeon.

To everyone's surprise, Lindo achieved nine distinctions for his nine subjects and set off for Stellenbosch University to begin his studies. I would meet the aspirant doctor in his third year after he had made the decision to drop out of medical school because of severe financial difficulties at home. His father had left the family and his mother had become unemployed. There were huge debts mounting up and loans were hard to come by.

His sister had started studying at Wits University and Lindo wanted her to have a chance as well.

I listened carefully as the young medical student, a mere three years away from achieving his dreams, slumped into my office chair in despair. He had outstanding fees from the past and no idea how to pay for the current year. Even with this sense of duty to his family, Lindo was teaching disadvantaged youth in Khayelitsha, the sprawling black township near the Cape Town airport.

After listening to Lindo tell his story, I re-told his journey in my regular Thursday *Times* column. Within a week, ordinary South Africans contributed enough money to wipe out his debts and cover much of his future medical education costs. Friends sometimes ask me: how do you choose the students you write about in your columns? Simple. A story is compelling if it has two elements – severe hardship and high standards. If you discover those qualities in a student, it is very easy to find money to fund their studies.

*　*　*

I had arrived at my Durban university office in shorts and a T-shirt. I asked the young woman behind the glass panel if I could have the keys to Room 325 (or whatever the number on the door was). She was mildly agitated: 'You people from Rentokil are always late.' They must have ordered this pest-control company to spray the office of the new chair in Curriculum Studies before I got there. There is something wonderfully entertaining about being misrecognised by your staff when you arrive for a new job. For the Indian secretary, the black man in working shorts could only be there to fumigate the place.

Years later, in 2000, when I was appointed dean at the University of Pretoria (UP), the same thing happened. I wandered down the corridors of the old *OpReg* (Education and Law) Building and knocked on the door of one of my future colleagues. 'Yeeeesssss,' she drew out the supposed greeting. Ours is a wonderful culture, in which a word like 'yes' could be both a greeting and a warning, as in 'what exactly do you want here?' Well, I told the short, young, white, blonde woman (I took this all in during a quick observation), I was simply exploring the lovely campus and wondered whether she would allow me to study something in this attractive place.

'This,' she said, now speaking slowly and emphatically, 'is a yoo-na-verse-sit-tee' and made it clear that 'you cannot just show up and want to study'. You must apply and you must have really good marks.

Well, I assured the young lecturer, my hands now rubbing each other as pleading people tend to do in our culture, I would work very, very hard if she would only give me a chance. She told me about UNISA as an option for people like me, the distance education university with its headquarters a short drive away on a hill in Pretoria.

I pushed for a while longer then thanked her for her time and made my way along the same corridor to her head of department's office. The white man literally jumped out of his chair when he saw me and offered everything from tea to fresh air as he skipped from one foot to the other. Unlike his colleague down the hallway, this head had been part of my earlier interview panel for the job so he knew that this was the incoming dean.

'Show me around,' I half-asked him as we sauntered down the corridor from which I came. At that moment, the young lecturer I had met earlier was coming towards us from the opposite direction. As she saw the two men talking and the ingratiation of her boss, she did some rapid calculations and realised that the black man she had spoken to earlier was not what he had pretended to be.

'Prof Dawie*?' she nervously addressed her boss in Afrikaans.

'Oh, Mika*, have you not met our new dean?'

Poor Mika grabbed the lower part of her dress and ran towards the women's toilet murmuring apologies as she fled.

It is not only white people who can misjudge a newcomer, for the same thing had happened a few days earlier when my family arrived at the main entrance to the gates of the University of Pretoria on Lynwood Road. UP had been a fortress of white intellectual and political authority for almost a century and was only now starting to appoint black men and women in senior positions. It was something new. I rolled down my car's window and told the two black security guards that I was the new Dean of Education and had been told to collect the key from them.

They both disappeared and I could see them having a good laugh. One returned and asked, 'Who did you say you are again?'

'I am Professor Jansen, the Dean of Education.'

'Well,' he said, stretching out his hand, 'I am Bishop Tutu.'

---

* Not their real names

Back in Durban in the early 1990s, I was about to get a baptism of fire as the new Chair of Curriculum Studies. The university itself was in constant turmoil. There were powerful factions organised around mainly labour issues and the personal griev- ances of a few influential lecturers. Campus was shut down and opened up in the same week as one or other demand fired up the protestors. Some of the issues, as always, were legitimate but others suggested a scorched-earth approach by the union representing the general staff. I was in a daze, having come from the serene environment of Stanford University, where heated intellectual exchange was the closest I got to any tension on a campus. Nelson Mandela was President of the Republic and it was at UDW that he inaugurated the first Presidential Commission of Inquiry into a public university.

I, however, had a job to do within the Faculty of Education and not long after my arrival was asked to stand as dean. The first thing I realised was that the standard of education at UDW was very low. I made that my singular purpose as dean – to make this the leading Faculty of Education in the country. How does one do that?

First, I noticed that there was a group of really smart young academics who themselves knew that the level of education was sub-standard. They were either studying towards doctoral degrees or about to achieve them. I made these very vocal young colleagues the heart of the academic transformation drive.

The most important next step was to have them achieve their doctorates, which they all eventually did. In that wave of aca- demic excitement, a number of other relatively young colleagues

88

who were in the support staff (student administration, laboratory assistance) also took the challenge and gained their PhDs. This for me was very revealing because the older colleagues clearly worked with a sense of the Indian caste system, which determined your station in life. The new advancement of young academics visited mayhem on this inherited system of castes. Some of these young colleagues became my doctoral students.

Then I put them through a vigorous postdoctoral programme of advanced scholarship support and training that included presenting their work at world conferences on education research, such as the American Educational Research Association (AERA). In a short period of time, books appeared, conference proceedings were compiled and articles were published in learned journals. New Master's programmes were created and postgraduate student numbers started to escalate because of the intellectual excitement generated within the faculty.

Outside the Education building, the campus was on fire. A student was shot and killed during one of the protests near the Law School. Millions of rands were illegally transferred from one of the university accounts. The local newspaper, in cahoots with some campus thugs, ran scandalous attacks on individual academics. One prominent international academic who got a senior position ahead of a local was serially harassed in his office and on his way home. The vice-chancellor's offices were routinely trashed. At that point, we established an Academic Staff Association of progressive scholars to push back against this thuggery that clothed itself in the language of transformation. It was not.

Back in the faculty, we pushed ahead with fundamental changes to the academic standard. In addition to generating a new cohort of doctoral and postdoctoral academic staff, we had to do two vital things: one, raise the standard of examination of new doctorates; and two, raise the standards for academic promotion. Both actions would create tremendous pushback.

There is a corruption in South African universities where a dissertation is circulated among friends and former students for examination. When examiner reports come in, the dissertation passes. The examination panel of the university is itself composed of like-minded people and before you know it, the student has a degree. I decided to read every dissertation the moment it was submitted for examination. I insisted that at least one, ideally two, examiners be international experts in the field. I changed the composition of the internal panel that received and made the final decision. In addition, every doctoral candidate had to defend their thesis in person, over a 90-minute period of examination. The students started to drop like flies and were given second and third opportunities to re-submit.

Supervisors were livid because the new rules of the game played them offside. The real tragedy for me was the student who had been misled by sub-par supervision. One otherwise timid supervisor lost his cool with me one day and said, 'You come here with your American ideas …' Actually, these were solid academic ideas about achieving the highest standards for the academy anywhere in the world. In due course, the message of high standards seeped through the system and the faculty enjoyed academic prestige among its peers.

Promotions were more personal and therefore more dangerous when it came to changing the rules. We pushed ahead. To become a lecturer, you ideally needed to have a doctorate in hand or be studying towards the apex of degrees in the academy. You needed to have academic teaching experience and already be publishing in one or more journals. Most of all, you needed to show signs of life – that ambition to become a leading academic in your field. If all those lights did not flash, we did not hire or advance an academic.

A senior lecturer, of course, had to do much more. Here, the standard was a cluster of publications, some of them in top international journals, in the years following the PhD. In education, that meant you were already drafting a manuscript for a book. By this stage, you needed to be the primary supervisor on Master's and doctoral degrees and several of your students should have been supervised to completion. You should be a regular presence in the right academic research conferences and should quickly be able to turn a conference paper into a solid publication. You should also have research teams organised around one or more research programmes with multi-year funding.

An associate professor would have already published scholarly books and could show how Book I (often a dissertation translated into book form) was different from Book II (with a leading international publishing house) and could show the draft for Book III (a single-authored text that broke new ground).

A full professor would have had a series of books published, an A- or B-rating from the National Research Foundation, a significant group of Master's and doctoral students, and be the leader of a well-funded research programme. The full professor would be a scholar with notable awards and prizes from around the world.

Implementing these new standards for promotion was really hard. For decades, the terms of appointment and promotion had been based on low standards. You really felt sorry for lecturer X who had dutifully completed committee duties, served at the behest of different deans, never missed a meeting – and so you promoted him so that he retired in a higher salary bracket than he would otherwise. Friends helped friends. Precedents were set that were hard to change and which laid down the rules for promotion in the years ahead. All of that came to a screeching halt. There were new standards and very few met them.

On the other side of the hill was the former white University of Natal. We tried to create synergies with our academic and research endeavours, but it was difficult. They knew what was happening at UDW but white institutional pride got the better of many of my colleagues there. Of course, they were superior, had better facilities and could trade on whiteness to carry their reputation. The truth was that the small academic enterprise at the University of Natal was not only academically stranded while UDW surged ahead, they were intellectually dominated by UDW's powerful staff complement when a government mandated merger required these Durban campuses to become one in January 2004.

This was probably the most important insight about the

South African academy that I gained on my return to the fray – the white universities, despite a century of racial privilege, were actually quite mediocre as academic institutions. True, there were pockets of excellence in some of the elite English universities, and an accumulation of formidable resources from the state in the historically Afrikaans universities, but they were mainly average when it came to their academic standing in the world.

I was now aware of a personal problem. Since my return to South Africa, I had thrown myself into the advancement of young academics and the development of institutions. This had become an 18-hours-a-day devotion that often included weekends. I travelled around the country, developing young scholars from Fort Hare in Hogsback, to Limpopo academics in Magoebaskloof. While I started my academic life with a promising curriculum vitae, I was losing momentum in my own research and publication agenda.

When I left UDW in 2000 and started as dean at the University of Pretoria, I did exactly the same thing – devoting every second to the development of young academics and rebuilding the Faculty of Education at UP, following the incorporation of a teacher's education college called Normaal Kollege Pretoria. This was a massive task since I had to decide which of the college staff to keep and which to retrench. So I assembled a team and interviewed every single staff member, of whom all but two or three were white South Africans.

I decided that the only thing that mattered was whether the college staff member could be developed into a strong university academic with research potential. This was hard to determine since college staff were hired for their capacity to teach future pre-primary and primary school teachers, something they did very well. I clearly needed some of these staff, since the college students were about to become part of the university's student composition, but something more was needed – the capacity to become strong academics.

We chose a small number based on this simple criterion and then the trouble started. One man came in with his wife, she being the lecturer who had not been selected. He was all brawn and bluster as he marched around my office. Picture this: the new black dean, a stranger in this very white place barely six years after apartheid, being threatened by this huge man who refused to take a seat. This could turn ugly.

I asked him why he was in my office when his wife, a confident woman, was the one affected by the decision. This was unacceptable, I told him, and asked the man to leave while I talked with his wife. Here, I was to confront one of those deeply ingrained habits of Afrikaner conservativism – the man still spoke for the wife, even if it was her job on the line. I was lucky at the time to have the full support of the university's rector and his team.

Once chosen, I needed to set a standard for these mainly young academics whom we had selected. So every day they had to show up for two hours and I trained them in the basics of educational research for months on end. This was hard for my colleagues, since college life and culture used to mean that you could go home at around noon, cook dinner for your family and have a restful evening preparing for the next day. While many staff appreciated the training in research to make them part of the new university, a few found this difficult and might even have resented this imposition on their time. I did not, however, expect God to be drawn into the fray.

One of the young married lecturers, a very good college lecturer in physics education, came to see me during one of those research training weeks. She was perfectly groomed, I remember, and in a soft voice told me across the table why this meeting was necessary. The previous night she had been on her knees and God had told her that she should stop attending my research training classes and give her full attention to her husband's needs and those of her children. Her family came first and I was interfering with the divine plan.

It helped that I was raised in a strict evangelical home, for this made me aware of how God could be invoked for all kinds of causes and calamities, whether real or imagined. So I told her that it so happened that I had also been on my knees the previous night and had been told she would be showing up with this cock-and-bull story. I explained to her how patriarchy works and that her husband needed to support her development as an academic and begin to play his part in the cooking and cleaning business. Needless to say, I lost that fight and I felt really sad that such a promising academic star could not see how her career would nosedive because of the short-sightedness of her man.

As dean, my job nevertheless was to create an excellent faculty and so even before I could begin incorporating the college staff, I needed to rationalise the existing academic staff. I asked for all their CVs and began plodding through them. I could not believe my eyes. Almost all the professors were white men and their CVs were among the weakest I had seen anywhere. How on earth had they become senior academics?

Soon, I understood how the system of patronage worked in the former white Afrikaans universities. They promoted each other on the flimsiest of evidence. Their closed academic networks in the other Afrikaans universities provided the references to enable these appointments. It helped, historically, if you were a member of the Broederbond (a secret organisation of exclusively Afrikaans-speaking Protestant white men, with the aim of furthering Afrikaner nationalism) and active in Afrikaner social and cultural circles. A political troublemaker or independent thinker stood no chance of promotion, whether in the nationalist academy, the church, the civil service or the public sector. Men did not hesitate to note their apartheid military duty in the CV. I wondered whether there was any awareness whatsoever about how such a CV would be read by the first black Dean of Education.

Quite apart from the political loyalties and social acquiescence that could be read in the CVs, the intellectual content and political ideologies of the slim research produced were not only outdated, but offensive. Outside of these universities, there was a comprehensive criticism that had developed in the liberal universities about *fundamental pedagogics* – the education philosophy that was used under apartheid to advance an apolitical view of education that sanctioned the authority of the state over citizens and of adults (teachers) over children in an authoritarian school system – and its evils but my colleagues simply could not see the problem. It was like asking a fish to question the water it swims in.

They needed to go. So once I had reviewed all the CVs, I called in the staff members one by one and explained what plans I had for the faculty and whether they would be able to adjust to the new agenda for change. With the older men, the professors with the scant CVs, I was more direct. I did not think they would make it in the new environment. I wanted to know if they would please leave so that I could use those personnel funds to hire new academics who would add to the racial and intellectual diversity of the faculty.

To my surprise, most of the men had already come to that conclusion – that the game was over. It would also, I suspect, be something of a relief to them. Taking orders from a black dean was as difficult as having, late in life, to make major intellectual and emotional adjustments to a new agenda. I asked the rector for a once-off funding dispensation which allowed me to pay the departing men the remainder of their contracts. This made the termination at least appear pleasant on both sides of the negotiating table.

We now had the opportunity to bring in brand-new academics from across South Africa and around the world and this enabled a deeper transformation of the new faculty. There were now two main groups of staff: new incoming academics with a broader repertoire of ideas and methods, and younger existing academics being prepared for the new research agenda of the faculty. But our elaborate plans for reinvigorating the place for academic excellence needed more money and it came from an unexpected place.

As I worked my way through the faculty finances, I discovered that there was upwards of R10 million hidden in the coffers. This was money accumulated under an extensive distance education programme, which at the time was still poorly regulated by the state and the funds of which were largely left alone by the central administration of the university. What to do with all this cash? Simple: invest it in a comprehensive staff development plan for all the academics, new and continuing, with the sole purpose of making them top research scholars.

This would require taking these colleagues out of South Africa and placing them abroad with leading researchers in their respective fields for up to one year. But this kind of adventure came with a high level of accountability. And so, at regular intervals, these academics, in which so much was being invested, had to present to their peers concrete evidence of their research progress. These accountability sessions came to be known as *Donker Vrydag* (Dark Friday) where the feedback was open and direct on each individual's progress.

The reason for these accountability sessions was based on a simple observation. All South African universities had one or other form of academic research support for staff. One of the most memorable carried the unfortunate name, Growing Our Own Timber or GOOT. Millions of rands were invested with little to show because the accountability checks were kept to a minimum. Somehow, universities thought that simply by pouring money into staff research development, academics would grow to become top researchers and scholars in their field. Much more was needed and one key element of any design strategy was accountability. What do you actually do with the resources invested in your development?

There were ripe pickings. A couple of the researchers worked with the future president of Yale University and came home to establish some powerful programmes in educational psychology, while retaining back-and-forth networks with this Ivy League school. Others changed their research direction completely from what they had done in their doctorates, producing scholarly books on a regular basis. Most of these colleagues became professors eventually and fully deserved those titles.

In a short space of time, the UP Faculty of Education became the leading producer of educational research in the country as our networks with top scholars spread around the world. It was also the first university to run a coursework-based doctorate in education combined with a full dissertation; the coursework was never recognised in the state subsidy but that did not matter, given the intellectual value of the teaching component. Scores of students graduated from this intensive programme in education policy, with teaching conducted by scholars like Richard Elmore of Harvard, Michael Fullan from the University of Toronto, Ann Lieberman from Stanford and Andy Hargreaves from Boston College.

When you set a high standard for your department or faculty or university, you must expect to lose some. Not everyone will be able to respond to the clarion call. Many academics see themselves only as teachers and simply cannot make the step up to become leading researchers. Others will surprise you and run with the new challenge. Invariably, the rising stars in your faculty are noticed by other universities and recruited for even higher positions. This is a double-edged sword. On the one hand, it is a compliment to your faculty that it has raised such stars and that they can contribute to education and development anywhere else in the country or, at times, in other parts of the world, but then you lose those academics to other institutions. At the same time, when lower-ranked universities, eager to boost their academic standing, promote a rising star prematurely, it is often the end of that person's career.

I have seen this happen so often – premature promotion. One such colleague had just completed his doctorate and become a professor at another university. That was the end of him. He no longer had something to work towards. He never again produced anything of value, let alone a scholarly book. In fact, he was never heard of again in the academy. Of course, I understood the need for status, recognition and more money. Those are not trivial pursuits in an academy that pays modest wages to its academic staff. But such short-term material pursuits can undermine long-term scholarly careers as it has done to so many of my most promising stars in educational research. What the inviting university has effectively done is to set the bar low and in the process, destroy a career.

When I became Vice-Chancellor at the University of the Free State (UFS) in 2009, it was now possible to do at an institution-wide level what was done at a department level (UDW) and faculty level (UDW and UP). As a university, we quickly adopted two main mission commitments, which we called the academic project and the human project. The human project was, in shorthand, to rebuild race relations on campus until such time that we could talk about human relations. That was not easy but we made huge strides in breaking down the deep animosity that made simple things difficult, like the racial integration of the university residences.

The academic project was also a challenge but the same formula would apply. Rebuild the professoriate. Bring in leading international scholars. Develop the smartest young scholars through an initiative we called the Future Professors Programme. Many other changes followed, such as the country's first university-wide compulsory core curriculum for undergraduate students. One of the more controversial measures taken was to raise the academic entry requirements for first-year students. I received a letter from a major political party accusing me of being racist. I returned a terse response, explaining that the real racism was not expecting black students also to do well in academic studies.

By this time, I was convinced that the reason UFS had one of the worst throughput rates in the country was that it took in the wrong students. Before I arrived, the university had experienced a severe financial crisis which led to staff layoffs. In response, UFS did what any other institution would do in such circumstances, and that was to spike the incoming student numbers and in this way, increase the revenue flow via tuition fees and the state subsidy. In the process, the standard of education dropped even more sharply.

I knew about this paradox from research that even for a university in rural South Africa, we could instead turn the numbers around by raising the academic standards for admission and thereby attract not only more students but the right students. Many of the top students from the province went to North West University, in part because of its more conservative, Afrikaans bearing, or to the University of Cape Town when it came to the top English schools of the country. Our marketing plan unashamedly sold the higher education standards as our rallying cry, something many parents were drawn to precisely because of the falling standards of the school system. And I personally joined the marketing teams to visit the top schools in the country, especially in Durban and Cape Town. After a slow start, our numbers increased rapidly for a simple reason – the quality argument won.

As at Pretoria, the new standard for academic promotions drew heavy fire from parts of the campus. To change the promotion criteria was to shift the goalposts in the middle of the game. The colleagues sitting in my office made it clear that they had consulted their lawyers. Their faces spoke of anger. Just before I came, they reminded me, Dr X or Y was promoted to associate professor with even fewer publications. None of that was contestable. I argued that becoming a professor against the new standards would give them even greater 'academic street cred' in South Africa and abroad. Some resigned immediately and were taken up by universities like UNISA.

One night, sitting alone in my office after everyone had gone home, I could not help smiling. When I arrived, my colleagues made me aware of the fact that there were murmurs on and around the campus that with my appointment 'the standards were going to drop'. Irony of ironies, the standards had gone up – and they did not like it.

Set a goal – then move heaven and earth to get there

Saloshna Vandeyar was one of the most determined young academics I had ever met. When I decided to elevate the scholarship of the youthful bunch of potential academic stars at the University of Pretoria, she stood out. Saloshna was married, a mother, and at least one of her children struggled with disability. None of that hampered her fierce desire for academic success. She attended every workshop and handed in every development assignment ahead of time, determined to get feedback. Unfortunately, she, like most of her colleagues, had done her PhD at Pretoria under some very mediocre senior academics. When I told the group (after reading some of their theses) that they should take their dissertations back to the registrar and say there was a mistake, Saloshna would have done that if it were possible.

So she started from scratch with the goal of moving from lecturer to professor. I had never seen someone throw everything into her academic career. Before long, she raced up the ranks to full professor, became director of her own Centre for Diversity and Social Cohesion, and chair of the Research Committee. After writing a book with me as second author, *Diversity High: Class, color, culture and character in a South African high school* (2008), she raced off to publish some of the most impressive publications on education, race and inclusion. In no time, the accolades poured in, including several international awards for outstanding scholarship from the premier research academies in the world. She had set herself a simple, singular goal and put everything into achieving what she set out to do.

✻   ✻   ✻

I was always competitive. It started with soccer. My schoolboy team was Hellenic in Cape Town and the only reason I chose this Greek-named franchise was because all the other friends in my primary school class chose Cape Town City and I wanted to support another team out of a sense of contrariness. It hurt badly that my Bible-believing parents would not allow me to go to Hartleyvale or one of the other stadiums of the ungodly on Friday nights or Saturday afternoons to watch the games. I would have to hear my friends recall goals scored or saved every Monday morning. But I was in there, competing to win.

When my teachers lit the academic fire under me, I also became competitive in tests and examinations. There were three other high school students in my grade who were really smart and I worked hard to compete with them. They always seemed to do better and that only motivated me to study harder than Alan Newkirk, Heather Augustine and a quiet girl in the

Afrikaans class. Strangely enough, I never thought of competition as a bad thing. Rather, I saw it as a way of bringing out the best in me, as stretching my own talents. When I was the first student in my high school class to gain a first-class pass, that energised me to continue to do better.

After my experiences of Cornell and Stanford, I had the confidence and the content to compete, but there was an added edge to the commitment to excel. I was now aware of the fact that re-entering South Africa meant that I had to compete within a highly racialised society. I knew that the decks were stacked in favour of white academics at the resource-rich universities. It soon became clear that I had an important advantage – I did not owe my academic attainments to any of them. I was truly independent.

South Africa has a strange culture in that you never quite outlive the influence of, and the obeisance due to, your supervisor. The person who supervised you somehow has an abiding hold over your progress if not also your destiny, like a guru in Indian culture. Some of my colleagues in Durban even call the supervisor the guru. This is good and bad – good in the sense that it signals respect and gratitude for supervision; bad in that you never grow up and away from the influence of your supervisor. 'She was Wally Morrow's student,' or 'He was Owen van der Berg's student.' I found that unpalatable.

I belonged to none of them and that independence meant a lot to me because I owed nobody anything in the South African firmament. As a young black academic with credentials from outside the South African system, I would, however, feel my outsider status. These mainly white academics had their own established networks, their own internal languages and their own conferences, such as Kenton-upon-something. I was not invited to any of those events when I returned home in 1991. I did not speak the language of Bernstein and Bourdieu, which still seem to thread through every single paper of these English university academics. I was certainly working outside the conservative ideologies spouted by my Afrikaans colleagues when they routinely cited the godfathers of fundamental pedagogics like Van der Stoep and Landman. When the Spencer Foundation (an organisation that investigates ways education might be improved) liberally supported doctoral studies at the white English universities, a discussion was held about whether to include me and my faculty at Pretoria; the decision was to exclude. So I found myself stranded as a young academic but remained determined to pursue my independent research and set my own standards for scholarship.

I did this over the years by creating my own research teams with their own identities in Durban, Pretoria, the Free State and now Stellenbosch, and I built formidable funding opportunities around these programmes.

When Tyler Perry made his speech at the 2019 BET Awards, I thought the brother was talking to me: 'While everybody was fighting for a seat at the table … I said, "Y'all go ahead and do that. But while you're fighting for a seat at the table, I'll be down in Atlanta building my own." Because what I know for sure is that if I could just build this table, God will prepare it for me in the presence of my enemies.' I knew exactly what the movie mogul was saying.

We built that table by planting strong research programmes and capacities through institution building. But this investment in building strong faculties came at a personal cost to my own research.

It is the case that I always kept an active research programme around my own interests in the politics of knowledge. But it was hard to convert those activities into substantial publications when I was running a faculty, let alone a whole university. I started to invest more time in my own research even as I invested in institution building. With the advice of colleagues, I decided to test the waters via the one system that offered a more-or-less objective account of your scholarship and that was the rating system of the National Research Foundation (NRF). You are on top of your game as an A-rated scholar ('leading international researcher') and fairly competitive as a B-rated scholar ('internationally acclaimed researcher'), while a C-rating ('established researcher') is certainly respectable compared to no rating at all. For younger scholars, the apex rating is a P ('prestigious awards') and then a Y ('promising young researchers') for competitive but less accomplished academicians.

After a long process, I got a B. It was okay, I suppose, but I wanted what only a few researchers in South African universities had achieved – an A-rating. At that time, very few non-science scholars got this rating and nobody in education had. In the process of participating in this rating exercise, I discovered two other surprising things – teaching counts for nothing, and institution building or community development even less so. The only thing that mattered was the depth, quality and focus of your research as adjudged by your national and international peers. The A-rated scholars were, for the most part, people who invested only in themselves, though there were notable exceptions.

So I made a change to my work habits because I wanted to be the best. I took a year off between UP and the UFS and returned to my old university, Stanford, on a Fulbright Fellowship for Senior Scholars. In that year, I wrote my first major scholarly book but its origins lay on the main campus of the University of Pretoria.

During my time as dean at UP, I would often find myself frustrated with the deep conservatism of the institution, the authoritarian behaviour of my seniors and the often outright racist or sexist actions of some academic and administrative staff. I would vent my frustration after another negative episode during the weekly meetings with the vice-rector (the preferred term in the Afrikaans universities for the deputy vice-chancellor of the English universities), to whom I reported as dean. I was fortunate to have mostly outstanding men (they were all male) as my senior colleagues in Die Skip (The Ship), the administration building that housed the rectorate.

One of my reporting vice-rectors, another black man, was not very helpful because he himself struggled openly, or so it seemed, with the whiteness of the institution. Before I could rant, he would offload his own frustrations with the place. One day, I came for our weekly meeting and he took off: 'Bra J, here they treat me like a baboon!' At that very moment his mobile phone went off to the tune of 'Bobbejaan klim die berg' ('Baboon climbs the mountain'). That was the end of the meeting for I simply could not compose myself for any serious interaction after that. I completed my laughing spell in the men's toilets next to the elevators of the building.

But Professor Chabani Manganyi was different. When he was assigned as my reporting vice-rector, I found a genuine mentor. A clinical psychologist by profession, Chabani was a deep thinker and every offensive episode or troubling observation would be the subject of long hours of analysis and discussion. I really looked forward to these regular engagements, which had less to do with the latest *opdrag* (instruction) from on high and more to do with things like the nature of knowledge and the problem of authority.

One day, I was particularly incensed and began venting even before we had completed the usual greetings. Chabani always reacted slowly and spoke deliberately. He let me rant. When I was done, he said to me, 'You know, JJ, you get angry before you think.' That was a turning point, a powerful learning that altered my way of thinking about a problem.

Chabani's brilliance was that he demanded, in his soft manner, that you ask questions about the behaviour itself, rather than allow offensive human actions to entrap you in unproductive cycles of anger. Where, he would ask, do you think the racists and the murderers under apartheid went? They did not vanish into thin air. They are still with us and among us. Our assumption that 1994 was a clean break with the past was, of course, nonsensical. People's ideas, emotions, beliefs and commitments did not simply switch on and off with Mandela's release from prison or the advent of our new democracy.

Chabani gently nudged me to study one of his abiding intellectual concerns, the psychology of the defeated. These were the white South Africans and the regime that had carried them. How does a whole group of people deal with the sudden loss of the power with which they had lorded over the majority for centuries and, just like that, it is gone? Or so we think. I was completely intrigued by the elegance of the question and excited about the pursuit of its resolve.

Of course, Chabani swung his sharp analytical sword both ways. One of the most complex traumas that he studied was the first crowd necklacing, in 1985, of a suspected apartheid police informer, Maki Skosana, subsequently found to be innocent. Where did the people who killed this innocent woman go? They are among us, Chabani would remind me.

In June 2007, with 10 academic months to do nothing else but think and write, I landed at the airport in San Francisco after a long transatlantic flight with a connection from New York to the West Coast (those added five to six hours can destroy any soul), collected the hired car and set off for my rental apartment. After a quick shower, I opened my laptop and started to write the story of how young white, Afrikaans-speaking South African students come to inherit powerful knowledge about a past they themselves did not experience. Chabani had, in the space of a few years, taught me to think and write reflexively and to challenge my own understandings of the young students whom I was privileged to teach and to lead. I did little else in those months than read, write, eat and sleep, for the book project had transformed my understanding of the white students at UP; their fears, anxieties and hopes were my own. One weekend, in the dead of night, I stopped writing. I was emotional and alone. These historical enemies were my people, I realised for the first time in my life.

The book, *Knowledge in the Blood: Confronting race and the apartheid past*, was published by Stanford University Press in 2009. During that time, my scholarship improved, my book won awards and I was gearing myself to prepare for my next NRF rating application. But I had learnt a tough lesson from friends in the natural sciences who knew the rating system well: you only apply when you are absolutely sure you are ready and that you have done the hard work necessary. While *Knowledge in the Blood* won prizes I could never imagine, including a handsome cash award from the British Academy for the Social Sciences and Humanities, I wanted to do more before a fresh submission to the NRF.

One of the most valuable lessons I had learnt about scholarly books was from the A-rated historian Charles van Onselen. Charles often made the point to me and the young academics at UP that in laying out your academic career, you need to understand the difference between your first book, your second book, your third book, and so on. In other words, you set the standard for your achievements progressively higher as you go along in your academic journey. Now I knew that *Knowledge and Power*, my first book, published in 1991, was a trial run. It was not very well-composed and would not win awards but it got me started. This was a book I'd edited and while it took an enormous effort to bring and hold together such a diverse span of authors, many of whom were writing an academic chapter for the first time, it held little value in the assessment of my scholarship as a first-time editor. But I would not have been able to do a second book if I had not sharpened my teeth on the first book.

In between *Knowledge and Power* (1991) and *Knowledge in the Blood* (2009), I had written for a broader audience I was serving – South Africans who read my popular weekly columns in *The Times*. As a public commentator on education, via the newspaper column as well as radio and television, I saw my role as being a public nuisance – to question silly ideas in education policy (like Outcomes Based Education) but also to push back against populist fervour (like corporal punishment). My editor at Bookstorm, a publisher in Johannesburg, suggested we pull together all these columns in a book, *We Need to Talk* (2011) which continues to sell well, and which was followed by *We Need to Act* (2013).

While these popular writings were, from my point of view, important as a form of public duty, public engagement and even public education, they meant little in the ratings game. I needed to get back into serious academic writing of books if I planned to improve my B-rating into an A.

This is probably the time to indicate why pursuing a treasured A-rating was so important to me in the South African context. It certainly was no vanity project; there are other labours that could satisfy such a superficial need. Anyone who read my first book, *Knowledge and Power*, would realise that my incentive was the advancement of black scholarship even as the partners in that project – as in all my projects – included white South African scholars. I was, and still am, deeply concerned that we have so few black South African researchers at the top of their game as A-rated academicians. How often would I attend award ceremonies and, time after time, the top researchers winning these awards were our white colleagues, not because they were smarter, but because of accumulated privileges from home to school to university and in society? The odds were stacked in their favour and while this continued, generations of students would think that intellectual brilliance resided only in white minds.

Of course, this was nonsense and nobody would make that public confession but the only way to counter such dangerous thinking in the post-apartheid period was for black academicians to step up to the plate and generate the kind of scholarship that demands the highest rewards and accolades. It is as simple as that. Those who know me would understand that this never was an anti-white stance but a social justice commitment. In academic attainment, the playing fields must also be levelled.

The problem is that black universities and black academics are taking shortcuts to academic excellence. Some institutions drop the standards for academic promotion, offering garbled logic about correcting the wrongs of the past. Others, as already discussed, recruit and advance the limited pool of black talent in an effort to demonstrate progress against the bleak picture of racial inequity in academic achievement. Even the national awards offered by the government to some black academics smack of desperation in the political game of allocating a set of awards called the National Orders. Schools even give awards for 'most progress', which makes sense but this is clearly to ensure that the national profile of achievers is not overwhelmingly white.

This is a mistake and it has happened before. For much of the 20th century, this is what Afrikaner institutions did in order to balance the scales when it came to white English universities. Instead of taking the long, hard route to achieving academic excellence, premature promotions were given to white Afrikaner men who displayed unquestioning loyalty to the apartheid state. We have seen this movie before, and as one colleague puts it – all nationalisms are the same, whether white or black.

It is this understanding of the academic project that has fuelled my work in the development of both black and white scholars over the years – that we must not compromise the academic standards in the South African academy for individuals or for groups of scholars. But there is another reason behind this drive to achieve the highest standards: it is not only about individual excellence but also institutional standing. Africa, to put it bluntly, needs strong universities.

This is why I have committed much of my life to institution building. Resources apart, there really is no difference between scholars at Cornell and Stanford, compared to those at UWC or Wits. Nothing. What sets them apart is that the top scholars on the other side of the Atlantic work in institutions that have three characteristics: they value the academic project above all else; they enjoy institutional stability; and they mobilise the resources that they have to attract and retain the best students and academics.

It is that second point – institutional stability – that concerns me greatly about the future prospects of the South African university and led to the book *As by Fire: The end of the South African university* (2017). As fires brought down residences, computer labs, libraries and science laboratories during the #FeesMustFall student-led protest movement around the country, I genuinely saw the end of our hard-won institutions – not so much the destruction of the physical buildings as the sustained assault on the very idea of the university. I made these points on the occasion of receiving an honorary doctorate of education from UCT in late 2019:

When you burn down things at a university because you're angry, you undermine what a university is for. When you hide and conceal artworks you don't like, you threaten the idea of a university. When you tell white students and colleagues that they cannot speak in the learning commons, you make a mockery of what a university stands for.

As by Fire was written as a warning, not as a defeatist manifesto, because we must recognise a trend in postcolonial history – our governments neglect their university assets and our students respond by destroying them. Travel throughout our continent and you will find that the African middle classes catapult their children to universities in Europe and North America and only the desperately poor remain in emaciated institutions, which open and close in response to one riot or protest after another.

What I have discovered is that the best universities in the world offer stable institutions where the brightest students can learn and where the smartest scholars can excel. South Africa, it seems, will not learn. We destroy on Fridays what we need on Mondays and then complain in one protest after another about the paucity of black professors. You do not fix that injustice by destroying the institutions you need for a powerful African scholarship that speaks to the problems of underdevelopment as well as the challenges of academic excellence.

To shift the mindset that excellence and equity are contradictory impulses, you simply have to look at the scholarly work of South Africa's leading researchers. Just before Bongani Mayosi died in 2018, I met with this brilliant scholar in his medical department suites at UCT. He was, as always, smiling and excited about his work. An Oxford-trained medical scientist, Bongani was doing world-class research in the area of poverty and cardiovascular diseases. It struck me that his scholarship earned him an A-rating by his peers in the rest of the world, while at the same time, that research was designed and executed in a context that addressed diseases of the African poor.

In the 2015–16 student protests, I could never understand the rehashing of old antagonisms of 'north and south' or 'the west and the rest of us' when it came to the conduct of research. What Bongani and many others demonstrated is how African leadership in research often brought young and experienced academicians from the rest of the world to learn together, share ideas and pool resources to address problems in context. These great African scholars did their research in a world of inter-dependence and co-operation, rather than dependence and inadequacy. That kind of disposition requires a mental and emotional mind-shift from one of inferiority to one where reciprocity becomes the norm in intellectual work.

Bongani Mayosi in medicine, Salim and Quarraisha Abdool Karim in HIV/Aids research and the African historian Ian Phimister became my contemporary role models for working at the cutting edge of one's disciplines and daring to break new ground in social and scientific inquiry. I knew that in the social sciences and education, the key was to produce a great book of scholarship and so I set upon this task. In the natural sciences, it is different; for scientists, a breakthrough article in journals like *Science* or *Nature* or *Cell* is enough to put you ahead in the game. For education scholars, it is as for sociologists and anthropologists: a great book.

I then wrote *Leading for Change: Race, intimacy and leadership on divided university campuses* (2016), which is a daring attempt to talk about the political emotions of university leadership, something about which little research had been done. That was followed by a study of interracial intimacies on university campuses titled *Making Love in a War Zone: Interracial loving and learning after apartheid* (2017) but neither of these books had the same impact in the scholarly community as *Knowledge in the Blood.*

In the meantime, I was humbled and surprised by the recognition and awards coming from other countries in various forms. Among the honorary doctorates, the one that really made a huge impression on me was from the University of Edinburgh. It was all light fun, with South African friends travelling from the Isle of Wight for the occasion, until the graduation party entered one of the most beautiful halls I had ever seen in my life. As with all things European, the sense of antiquity in the buildings, the beauty of the lighting and the imposition of the elevated graduation stage, the mass of people inside and the haunting music being played … I was overwhelmed by the enormous occasion.

As the main party walked slowly down the carpeted aisle, I remembered an incident at Heathrow the day before. The customs agent was a young black woman who, like all border officials everywhere, had a face that communicated a mix of boredom and irritation.

'What are you going to do in Scotland?' she asked me in monotonic syllables.

I piped up, 'I'm getting an honorary degree!'

Then she hit me. 'Oh, is that the one you don't have to work for?'

It was half-funny and I decided to enjoy the humorous part.

It was at this point in my career that I learnt you do not work for awards. You simply produce outstanding research and you publish that work in the right places and the awards will come. Too many young scholars are more worried about applying for one award after another and then find themselves repeatedly disappointed because they have not done the hard yards when it comes to doing outstanding research.

Probably the most serious unlearning that has to happen with young, ambitious academics is confusing quantity with quality. I understand how it happens. A lecturer is under pressure from her head of department to 'produce' more articles for a quick turnaround in research output. The head is in turn under pressure from the dean to 'up' the research units produced in his department to earn greater subsidy income. Every week, the dean meets with the deputy vice-chancellor for research where faculties are compared in terms of research productivity, and gets the message: we expect more from your faculty. It hurts a dean when her law or humanities faculty is compared to science and engineering, where the research graph goes upwards year after year. The deputy vice-chancellor's performance measurement by the vice-chancellor rests almost entirely on whether she is able to improve the university's slice of the pie when it comes to the research funding divided among 26 public institutions. It is a vicious game bereft of research integrity and explains the widespread academic corruption being reported in the world of scholarly publications.

It is important to focus on quality. The quality of the journal matters. The publishing house for your book matters. The originality of your argument matters. New knowledge matters. Rather spend five years writing a ground-breaking book than 'salami-slice' the small body of research for maximum outputs by putting different titles on the same work. You might win on the subsidy income but you will never become a great scholar in your field.

I was still at the University of the Free State when I made the decision to submit my work for an NRF rating in 2015. There were all kinds of risks associated with this move. No vice-chancellor had applied for rating while in the post. Only one or two had achieved A-ratings, like a one-time Rhodes University leader, but that was probably because of his laboratory science prior to assuming the vice-chancellorship. I had pushed the university academics hard on their research standing and promotions; they would no doubt be watching the outcome of my NRF application like hawks. True, I could probably get away with a good rating less than an A, since I was running a multi-campus university with my team. All of these considerations went through my mind but it was time for another reason – *set the example*.

So eventually I pressed the 'send' key on the online submission. As everyone who has done this knows, the waiting kills you. Self-doubt sets in. You talk yourself down in terms of expectations, to manage any disappointment.

Eventually, the A-rating came and I was relieved for myself but especially for my university. I wanted the institution to break free from its image as a rural university in central South Africa to one that for the first time had three A-rated scholars: Max Finkelstein in mathematical statistics, Melanie Walker in human development studies, and me.

So how did this happen? How is it possible to both lead a university and be productive as a researcher? This is what I did. Since my re-appointment as dean at UP, I realised that the only way I was going to live both my dreams – as a scholar and as a leader – was to negotiate 'time away' with my bosses. I could do the routines of data collection in the course of my daily work with outstanding senior staff in support, but writing requires disciplined time. Fortunately, the bosses agreed and I ensured that there was always one (or more) vice-rector who could continue the job at the level and intensity required. I also chose the time so that about three of the months away overlapped with dead time at South African universities (like November through January).

Those sabbaticals made all the difference and my California alma mater has become a wonderful oasis for a thirsty scholar. Two different Fulbright scholarships got me there and back, as well as a year at Stanford's Center for Advanced Study in the Behavioral Sciences. My 2020 Knight Hennessy Fellowship (during which I would teach world leaders once a week and spend the rest of my time thinking and writing) has been postponed due to the COVID-19 pandemic.

It was, however, not simply about 'being away' but also about 'being with'. Fundamental to advancing learning is being surrounded by really smart people with whom to test your ideas. This was one of the most important learnings on my journey – what matters more than anything in the trajectory of your career *is the company you keep*.

One of the most erudite scholars in the history of South African science is a friend called Wieland Gevers. Over the years, our paths have crossed often and we still work together as officials in the Academy of Science of South Africa. Before Wieland became a leading academic administrator at UCT, he was a world-famous medical biochemist. I was curious how a boy from Piet Retief in the old Transvaal achieved so much. It turns out his PhD supervisor was the Nobel Laureate Hans Krebs (remember the Krebs cycle from high school biology?) and his postdoctoral adviser was Fritz Lipmann, another Nobel scientist. Imagine working in the laboratories of these famous scientists and publishing with them in scientific journals. That's the secret – it matters, the company you keep, academically speaking, for they set the standard, create the environment and advance the careers of those in their space.

For similar reasons, I need to reunite on a regular basis with colleagues at Stanford to learn what else is happening in my field of interest. It has helped enormously to know what top scholars are thinking, reading about, teaching and writing. I need to be in an environment where the first thing a fellow researcher asks you is, 'What are you working on at the moment?' In other words, I need to be among people who set the standard, to which I too can aspire in the never-ending process of learning how to be a scholar.

Beware the riptide

No book has haunted me more than *The Short and Tragic life of Robert Peace*. The signs were everywhere that his was simply another black life whose outcomes would be predetermined by circumstances of race, poverty, drugs and violence. His father would die in prison for a double murder. But Robert's mother pushed back, working long hours in a kitchen and saving hard to get her son into good private schools, onto the water polo team and eventually, as a straight-A student, through the gates of the famed Yale University.

Robert Peace passed his degree with a double major in molecular biochemistry and biophysics while working in a cancer research laboratory. But what he concealed was that every time he returned to the ghetto of his birth in Newark, New Jersey, he continued a dangerous life of drug dealing. He died by the bullet, and right there in the ghetto the tantalising promise of reinvention ended.

A riptide is a powerful current that pulls a bather from the shore and eventually drags the unskilled swimmer below the waves to drown. In my learning journey, I encountered this riptide often – from the time I dropped out of university as a first-year student, to the moments I contemplated returning home from doctoral studies abroad. The riptide is ever-present and threatening, especially in the lives of young black students; it takes down many under the waves of a difficult life. I was lucky to survive and use those lessons from life and learning to guide many of my students safely to shore.

Sinoxolo Gcilitshana was not known to me but his school was. Oscar Mpetha High School was one of the worst schools I had visited in a long career of working with township schools to inspire learners in an assembly, to workshop teachers in a staff room, to advise a principal on leadership, or to encourage parents to become more involved in their children's school. This is what I do and who I am. In the process, I have known some of the best of schools like Mbilwi Secondary School in Thohoyandou in Limpopo or Menzi High School along the eastern seaboard or Mondale High School on the flats of Mitchells Plain. But I also saw the worst of schools and Oscar Mpetha High in Nyanga, Cape Town, was one of them.

I did not, therefore, expect a call from a history teacher at a very posh Cape Town school who was about to do something improper. The teacher told me that as an examiner in the recent matriculation examinations, she had marked the script of a student who had achieved the highest mark in Grade 12 history, almost 100 per cent. That young man was from Oscar Mpetha High School. Not possible, I remember telling myself; I know the school. My friend and collaborator, Molly Blank, a young American filmmaker had made a documentary about the school with the lovely double meaning of a title, *Testing Hope*. Shortly after making this film, one of the student stars in the show was brutally killed in this dangerous part of Nyanga, which borders a busy taxi-rank and where all kinds of illicit activities congregate, right next to the school. 'That is strange,' I told the informant, recalling my experience of the school. I promised that I would look into the matter.

At the time, I was vice-chancellor at UFS with some marketing resources to attract the best and the brightest to our university. I was also becoming more adept at using social media and so I started to search for the history whizz-kid Sinoxolo. A few phone calls later and we were connected. After congratulating the young man on his tremendous achievement, this was the interaction that followed:

JJ: What are you planning to do with your life?

SG: Well, Prof, I am on my way to Cape Town to get a licence to become a bus driver for Golden Arrow.

JJ: Okay, but would you not rather study further?

SG: I applied to UCT but was not accepted.

JJ: Would you consider studying at the University of the Free State for free?

SG: Yes, I would.

JJ: Please pack your bags and go to the bus terminus in the city; I will collect you at the stop in Bloemfontein. By the way, how did you get close to 100 per cent for history?

SG: Oh, my teacher was from Zimbabwe.

It was as simple as that. Sinoxolo travelled with another promising student from Delft, a socially and economically depressed area outside Cape Town, and they arrived in Bloemfontein early one morning. I brought them home, where my wife Grace prepared a sumptuous breakfast for the two matriculants. They looked positively scared, like all Cape Town people once they get beyond the mountains of Du Toitskloof Pass. After all, these two young men were on a long-haul bus overnight to a city they had never been to, for studies on a campus they would not have imagined ever coming to in their school years.

Sinoxolo adapted quickly. As with all first-year students, the jump from high school to university was a challenge but he settled into his new residence and would regularly swing by my open-door office for a quick chat.

Then it happened – the riptide began sweeping Sinoxolo away.

'What's up, brother?' I asked.

'Well, Prof, my dad left home for another woman. My mother and sister are alone in the shack. You know how dangerous it is. I am the man in the house now. I have to protect them. I am going to give up my studies and go home to Nyanga.'

As Sinoxolo spoke, I immediately recognised the riptide moment because I had seen and experienced it so often before. I told him that I understood the situation. I also made it clear that should he go back to Cape Town, his family would likely stay in that shack forever. Would he not think about it first before rushing home? I would like to speak to his mother, if he did not mind. If she agreed that he had to go home, I would arrange the return bus ticket.

So I called the mother. She was working at Cape Town International Airport. I explained the situation, the options available to her son and the long-term consequences. The mother was clear from the start: Sinoxolo should complete his degree first before coming back. That was the end of the story. The next time he would return home was for the coming university vacation.

Sinoxolo flourished at university. The academics were a challenge, given his overall poor schooling, but he passed, doing particularly well in history in his teacher education degree. In leadership, he excelled, going on to become the head of Khayalami House, a large male residence with a proud tradition. He regularly shared his wisdom on living and leadership on his social media pages. The students loved Sinoxolo for his humour, generosity and most of all his ambition to become the vice-chancellor of Wits University. I teased him often: 'Why Wits? I taught you to have standards!'

In the final year of Sinoxolo's undergraduate studies, I received a call from the acclaimed writer and former vice-chancellor of UCT, Njabulo Ndebele. Professor Ndebele now chaired the Mandela Rhodes Foundation and wanted to let me know what an impressive candidate Sinoxolo was and yes, he had been selected to become a scholar in this prestigious scholarship programme.

Sinoxolo would study towards a postgraduate qualification in the teaching of history, of course. I was deeply moved on hearing the news and called to congratulate the maestro. This was a world far removed from Golden Arrow Bus Service.

They say if you are patient and do not panic, and if you swim smartly, you can survive the forceful currents of the riptide.

*   *   *

Samantha Williams is from Lavender Hill, one of the turbulent areas of the Cape Flats where the army is sometimes deployed to put a lid on constant deaths from gang violence. The only child of a single mother who works shifts at Game department store, Sam was the head girl of my old high school and a top academic performer.

Few students from Steenberg High School go to university and few who enrol go on to obtain a degree. After working with schools across the country, I decided it was time to go home and open up opportunities for students from Steenberg. Of the first group of five students recruited, the riptide took down four of them.

Samantha was in the second group and she decided to study law at UFS. She was placed in the most prestigious women's residence on campus, Roosmaryn, where the academic highfly-ers congregated. It was going to be tough for this young woman from the Flats more than a thousand kilometres away. When she went home for vacations, Samantha stayed indoors. The sound of bullets and the rumours of another gang fight could termi-nate a promising career during a simple trip to the nearby shop. But Samantha fought those riptides and eventually got the LLB degree, despite the heavy odds against her.

What I did not expect was that Sam would achieve distinctions in virtually every one of her law degree subjects and therefore graduate with distinction. Very few students ever accomplish this feat.

Despite such excellent results, there was another riptide to negotiate – getting a legal internship in the competitive environment of Cape Town's bustling metropole.

It had been clear to me for some time how school and university graduates get ahead in the city of my upbringing. It depends almost entirely on where you went to school. That, in turn, depends on who your parents are, where they went to school, and of course how much they earned. If you went to the private school Bishops or the quasi-private public school 'Bosch, you were set for life. You could well be the biggest idiot in your class but your dad only needed to make one call to an old boy from the same school or the business partner in a private equity firm and you were good to go. It's called cultural capital but I prefer the more honest term: racial and class privilege.

Samantha did not fit the bill. She is an unassertive woman, soft-spoken, from a disadvantaged school, living in a crime-burdened neighbourhood as the child of a single mother. Yes, I know, the LLB with distinction should carry her through but as my co-author Samantha Kriger and I show in our book, *Who Gets in and Why: Race, class and aspiration in South Africa's elite schools* (2020), access to prized institutions is anything but meritocratic – it depends on who you are, where you live and how much you can pay.

In the everyday language of the Cape Flats, Samantha was *sitting at home doing nothing*. She picked up the phone and explained to me that she desperately needed opportunities for an internship and that clerking with a recognised law firm would change everything. It was time to take on the powerful tide with this smart young law graduate and so I made five calls to friends within my own networks to explain the situation. Within days, Samantha got calls to come for interviews and after some time, she had options with top law firms in the country.

It is an idea I have put to several black (and white) friends who have achieved great things in their respective fields (law, education, medicine, finance, estates) – to form a network of expertise that mentors and directs young graduates without the social and cultural capital to gain access to prized opportunities in the labour market. Samantha, no matter how determined, could not swim alone, for those cross-cutting currents would have ripped away any of the enthusiasm and motivation that might have come with a competitive degree.

No student I know has had to swim against more riptides than Nozimanga Bonje. Nozi, as everybody calls her, was raped as a young teenager by a cousin but her mother would not press charges because the rapist's father put bread on their shared table. She was asleep with her younger brother when Nozi heard blows and screams in the shack where the family lived. She would witness her father beat her mother to death, after which she was told to clean up the blood. It is a trauma that the young child would never overcome. The alcoholic father went to prison, and on his release, the man would harass his daughter for money.

Few young women would ever recover from the brutality
of rape and the first-hand witnessing of the murder of their
mother at the hands of their father. Nozi has definitely struggled. At one stage, she lived in a self-made shelter on the streets.
By some incredible stroke of luck, her path would cross that of
the headmaster of the prestigious Grey College, a boys' high
school in Bloemfontein. Johan Volsteedt gained fame as a great
principal and sports master through whose hands some of the
nation's best cricketers and rugby players passed. But Johan also
did something for the less fortunate – he ran holiday schools on
the grounds of Grey for children from disadvantaged schools.
This is how he met the academically talented but socially for-
lorn Nozi Bonje.

Sensing her academic potential, Johan got Nozi transferred
from a township school to the elite girls' school, Eunice High
School which, like Grey, bordered the main campus of the
University of the Free State. Nozi excelled and registered at UFS
for a science degree with human genetics as her major. Nozi did
well and qualified to continue her studies towards an honours
degree in genetics and get her first job at a biogenetics firm.

But how would we fund her studies? Johan brought the young
woman to my office one day and I asked Nozi to tell me her
story. By the time she was done, I had to excuse myself for I was
so emotionally overwhelmed I could not continue the interview.
It was not only the cruelty visited on a tender life that broke me;
it was the calm composure with which she shared her life story.
I decided to tell her story, with permission, through my weekly
column in *The Times*. I included her student account details at

the bottom of the column.

The money came in quickly and Nozi was funded for the duration of her studies. One woman had a debit order for R1 000 run for seven years to support Nozi. A pensioner from Wentworth (a depressed township outside Durban) called to ask if her R20 that was left over after accounting for her monthly pension might help. Untold generosity, because the story was so compelling on its own, but also because it spoke to the harsh, unforgiving contexts in which post-apartheid youth still lived their lives.

The riptide threatened all the time throughout Nozi's life as a student. The anniversary of her mother's death would often disable her emotionally. A sudden and unexpected recall of traumatic memory would fell her. She worked hard to forget and she sought help through counsellors all along her learning journey. Church became a fixture of her life. My wife, as well as Johan, among others, invested many hours mentoring Nozi and trying to give her the best possible life as memory tried to bring her down below the raging waters of the riptide.

Every student experiences that riptide in a different way. For Sinoxolo, it was primarily about overcoming the fear of the women in his family being exposed to danger; he needed reassurance that his mother and sister would be secure in the future. For Samantha, it was the sheer hardship of being raised by a single mother in a dangerous neighbourhood. For Nozimanga, it was about dealing with traumatic memory of what happened in the past. She needed the guardrails of mentors and friends to keep her focused on her studies even as the weight of history hung on her back.

What I have learnt about riptides is that while they affect young people in varying degrees, there are common characteristics of students who overcome these powerful forces. All of them are determined human beings. In other words, there is something within them, a kind of resilience that takes on the fight, even in the direst of circumstances. Which brings me to another favourite quote of the famous immunologist Louis Pasteur: *'Let me tell you the secret that has led me to my goal. My strength lies solely in my tenacity.'*

That willingness to fight is either present or it is not. How young people achieve that tenacity is not entirely clear to me but it helps to be stubborn and not to accept what seems to be a lost situation.

But I have also learnt that nobody succeeds by fighting alone. Tenacity can be built by surrounding yourself with tough swimmers, to extend the metaphor, those experienced in charting life's difficult waters. This means reaching out to people who can help and accepting the offers of those who want to assist.

Those fighting resources to taking on the tides are also different for different students. Some find great comfort and strength in a life of faith. I know many students who would not have survived were it not for the mid-week cell group from church or the Word received on a Sunday morning. Others find their will to succeed in social, cultural or political organisations. Being with people who share a common purpose can make a considerable difference in a student's adaptation to university and in their success in the classroom. The idea is not to be alone but to reach out to those who can help lift your spirits and focus your efforts as the tides change around you and threaten the course of your life.

Riptides can come out of nowhere. How often have I seen a student cruise through their years of study and then, without warning, there is a telephone call from home. Your father was diagnosed with a deadly cancer or your sister died in a car accident or the family was evicted for non-payment of rent. For many students, the bottom falls out. There is bewilderment and sometimes guilt for not having been there when the crisis came home. When one student at UFS found out that his romantic partner was in a critical situation in ICU, he went to the roof of the medical building and jumped to his death. We are not all wired in the same way. An unexpected riptide can instantly wreak havoc on the personal lives of students.

That is why more and more universities invest in counsellors, psychologists and other healthcare professionals. It is tough being a student under ordinary circumstances; it is even more difficult for students who come from broken homes and poor communities and schools that did not prepare them adequately for the rigours of university life.

The point of this chapter on riptides is that as a student, you are not a helpless victim. You can reach out for help. You should identify the resources around you. You can manage the currents by taking firm decisions, the most important of which is not to give up.

Which brings me back to the intriguing story of Robert Peace who, despite his tremendous talent, continued to deal in drugs which eventually led to his brutal killing on his knees in the family home. To be sure, there are many readings of the Peace story, both sympathetic and critical.

One reading is that Peace was the victim of forces much more powerful than himself that had their roots in slavery and dispossession, and the failure of America to recognise and make restitution for a history of racism. In this narrative, you cannot blame the individual for the systemic conditions that make black men, in particular, the targets of police brutality and an unfair justice system. Robert Peace was therefore a product of a racist, capitalist system and under those conditions, you do not blame the victim.

To be honest, there is much in such a sociological account of black lives that I can and do relate to. I teach on the systemic nature of injustices and how the past lingers in the present. I get that.

My problem is that Robert Peace is still dead.

In my theology, I cannot give up on the individual because the system is oppressive. In my sociology, I do not render people as hapless victims but as social agents, even under the most repressive conditions. And in my politics, I dare not give up on hope and the possibility that through individual and social activism, we change the conditions of our oppression.

What all of this means is that Robert Peace had the capability to make decisions — such as the decision to go to university and successfully complete a Yale degree. That was not easy but he did it. What he also actively decided to do, sadly, was to continue in the drug trade. However powerful that riptide, and it was, Robert Peace could decide which path to take. Surely he knew, following the life of his father, that the path of drug dealing inevitably leads to incarceration and even death. A Yale graduate with great capabilities made a wrong decision and with that, the tireless work and the desperate dreams of his mother were shattered.

The riptide took him down.

Find your passion – and pursue it

It happened so often I started to become irritated. Two parents would be sitting in my office with their child asking for help. Sonja is determined to become a teacher but her ambitious parents have other ideas. There is no money in teaching and does she know how difficult it is to manage children in this day and age? I was always puzzled why the parents would run this particular line of argument past me, an education man, without realising I might be offended. Nevertheless, the parents made it clear that she would be a great lawyer or chartered accountant and make a good living. Could I please speak sense into her head?

At this point, I would turn to Sonja and gently ask her, 'My child, what would you really like to do?' (Warning: the 'my child' appellation is only appreciated in Afrikaans culture.) Sonja would, with great hesitation and often in tears, tell me how since she was a child she used to line up the teddy bears and dolls in her room and teach them. She always wanted to work with little children. She even teaches Sunday School at her church and really enjoys it. I keep one eye on the parents, look-ing for the hint of an eye roll.

When Sonja is done, I turn to the parents and make the point that in my experience, it is important that a student follows her passion because it is her choice of career, that she needs a reason to get up every morning and that she alone carries the consequences of one or other choice of degree.

The parents would grumpily thank me, the family would take off and months or even a year later, Sonja would be back in my office. By now, Sonja had developed the confident voice of a determined undergraduate student. She had passed all her modules for the law degree and is well on her way to gradua-tion. But I feel nothing, Professor. I'm just going through the motions; it is not my passion. Sonja then restarts her first year but as a teacher-education student.

If there is something I have learnt in life about learning, it is this simple lesson – find your passion and pursue it.

The Sonja story has a flip-side, however. Not every student who comes to university knows in advance what they wish to study. The bad news is that South African universities force stu-dents into making a choice on day one as to whether they will study engineering or journalism or medicine. This works for a student with an early determination to pursue a particular profession. But many young people need more time to decide.

That is one reason I prefer the liberal arts degree of some overseas universities where a student studies broadly in the first two years before choosing a direction, like medicine or the arts. I also like the idea of a broad-based common core curriculum so that all students are introduced to big questions in astronomy, economics, law, ethics, media and the sciences. In this way, a student becomes educated before they are trained in a specific field.

This was the idea behind the first compulsory, campus-wide core curriculum, which we implemented at UFS. At first, students hated this course, as one told me: 'I am here to do urban planning and nothing else.' Later on, many (not all) students came to understand the value of a broader education, rather than the narrowness of an early disciplinary specialisation.

To students who are undecided, I often suggest they do a broad-based BA degree. It is still the best guarantee of an all-round education if done at a good university with the best undergraduate teachers. Over the years, I was told by seasoned professionals in different fields that they would prefer a student not start by studying for a degree in a specific field like journalism or media studies but rather that they be educated more broadly in history, anthropology, sociology and politics. In this regard, I cannot forget the wisdom of the then head of the Johannesburg Stock Exchange, Russell Loubser, when I first met him: 'You educate them, Professor; we will train them.'

On reflection, I too did not plan to become a teacher on leaving high school. I was fascinated with biochemistry as a field and thought that a path to pharmacy might come of that. I certainly did not imagine it was possible for a child from Steenberg to become a professor; certainly not. But since I needed the state bursary to finance my studies – under apartheid, that bursary was only granted to black students if you declared that you were planning to become a civil servant like a teacher, librarian or police officer. So when I got my BSc degree I decided to teach for a few years to pay off the bursary and then proceed from there to choose a science profession. But on the very first day that I stepped into the biology classroom at Vredenburg Senior Secondary School (only the white schools were allowed to be called high schools), I knew this was my passion – on day one.

There was, to be honest, also a broader passion and that was to serve in rural communities outside of my familiar and comfortable home of Cape Town. A mix of adventure, service and evangelical mission fuelled this desire to leave home as a new graduate. So when the list of vacancies were advertised, I consciously chose to teach in faraway rural areas. This was my Zuma Year, as the health sciences students call it, before there was a Zuma Year. You had to give three options in the application. I remember applying to a high school in Beaufort West, another in De Aar and of course, Vredenburg. In due course, I was informed that I was going to South Africa's west coast, where I would be teaching children from that small town and the surrounding fishing areas of Saldanha Bay, Paternoster, Laaiplek-Veldrif and Lambert's Bay, among others.

It was a strange situation. Many of the students were about my age, for an interesting reason. This was the first high school in this not-white area. Before, when children finished primary school, those parents who could afford it sent their children to live in hostels at distant high schools like Schoonspruit in Malmesbury about 100 kilometres away. The rest went to work in places like Sea Harvest in Saldanha Bay. How do I even begin to command the attention of young adults with work experience who thought I could be their pal? My response was to play the role of the take-no-nonsense teacher, the tough guy. More timid teachers used to send their troublemakers to me for a workover. It was through my teaching, however, that I decided that I needed to impress these young minds.

I remember the transformative moment well. I was teaching the concept of pH, that measure of the acidity or alkalinity of a solution. The students were attentive, all of them. And as I explained, I could almost read the moments of understanding in their faces, some more quickly than others. Right then, a powerful emotion gripped me: if I can make complex things simple for learning, imagine what change could happen in the learning and lives of these children from mainly working-class and impoverished homes? It was then, after four years of a BSc degree, that I realised that teaching would be my passion. I could make a real difference in this way.

Once I found my passion in biology (now called life sciences in schools) teaching, I threw everything into it. I prepared for one lesson for hours on end. I would think of three different ways of teaching the life cycle of the fern or the Krebs cycle in cellular respiration. For each lesson, I thought of an experiment or practical of some kind so that students could see and feel their way through the biological sciences. This was important to me since I had very little if any experience of doing science 'practicals' at high school. It was all theory and you read the experiments in the textbook.

This caused me serious harm. When I first saw a microscope in Professor Kristo Pienaar's botany class at the University of the Western Cape, I had no idea what to do with this thing. During the very first lab, and to the amusement of my class-mates, I tried to look through the wrong end of the microscope as if this was an astronomy class. My biology students, I was determined, would learn to do science by handling a pipette and burette doing titrations, and a scalpel during the dissection of a rabbit.

The rabbit decision landed me in trouble at my next appoint-ment, Trafalgar High School. A Muslim student asked me if he could speak to the media about his ethical concerns regarding dissections. I was mildly apprehensive but since I encouraged free speech and open debate in my classrooms, of course he could speak to the media. Big mistake. The local paper came breathing down my neck, followed by the SPCA. It was the first time I had made front-page news in any medium. My argument was straightforward: the children at Bishops and Westerford do dissections that prepare those students for university education; why are you picking on a black school with none of the fancy laboratories and materials that they have? I was incensed by the double standards.

My passion was to teach biology the way I wish I had been taught and so I bought my own biological materials (and rab-bits) from my meagre salary. I also borrowed science equipment from friends at UCT and from Mr Adriaanse, a fellow bio teacher at nearby Harold Cressy High School. To make these experiments manageable, I choose a week in the term in which my dedicated classroom would be transformed into an active laboratory of 12 stations, each with a different practical task, and the students would move from one setting to the next until they had completed all the assignments.

Back at my west coast school in Vredenburg, I was on a roll. I taught from the first day of school in January, which my colleagues found amusing. In those days (and in many township schools to this day), it took at least three to six weeks, if not longer, to allocate students to classes and classes to teachers. Subject combinations depended on teachers available and, of course, student demand. It was a mess that I could never understand but since I was a junior teacher straight out of university with a science degree but no teaching qualification, I knew my place. When you eventually got your allocated classes, it was time for the annual athletics day and so more weeks slipped into oblivion. This was the first time I realised how white schools always performed better than black schools. It was not only the unequal resourcing under apartheid; it was also the lack of academic planning by people who should have known better.

I taught my allocated class like a madman. Every second counted. Every episode of teaching was followed by a short homework assignment as well as regular tests. I literally begged the students to come in on Saturday mornings so that I could revise the work of the week or do experiments for which a 40-minute period, or even a double period, were ill-suited. This did not work well since many students lived outside of Vredenburg, travelling on school buses from places like Hopefield or hiking back and forth each morning from faraway places since their parents could not afford hostel accommodation. That is how I lost one of my star students, Horingtjie. He was an A student in biology and to my horror, I learnt that the quiet and hardworking Horingtjie hiked a lift to school one day on the back of a bakkie that overturned and killed him. It was a sadness that stayed with me for a very long time.

My energy for teaching did not subside on a Friday and so my hostel students were the guinea pigs on the weekends. After a nine-to-noon teaching session, we would play rugby together – soccer did not enjoy much of a following in the rural areas. Students would find great pleasure in having some of the heavies like Avril Williams come storming towards my position at centre to try and level the bio teacher with the ground. I was young and tough and gave as good as I got. It was fun.

With the athletics season upon us, I was given the middle-distance athletes for training. The school athletics day did the job of winnowing out the more serious athletes from the rest and suddenly I had my team of elite boy athletes for the 800-metre, 1500-metre, 3000-metre and 5000-metre races. As in academics, I was passionate about excellence and so I put the boys through the toughest training regime for high school athletes. Every Saturday morning in the athletics season, we would run from the gates of the school in Vredenburg along a tarred and then gravel road to Paternoster on the coast, a distance of about 16 kilometres. Some of the students would dive into the ice-cold water and then run back.

During the week, the same intensive training took place on the school grounds. It was also on school days when we discussed tactics such as when to hang back in second or third place in a competitive race, how to read a pace-setter and of course, when to line up for the sprint about 150 metres out in the middle distances.

At the Boland and the Cape interschool competitions, we won every single one of those middle-distance races and sent those students to the national school championships. The next year, the senior teachers decided to give the middle-distance training to one of their own. It was a bitter pill to swallow for a newbie teacher and we did not win a single race in the following year's competition.

I continued to teach hard. Right at the beginning, I learnt an important lesson about teaching and learning. After two weeks of intensive teaching at the start of the school year, I gave a class test. The results shocked me. It was heart-breaking. Despite my best efforts, few students passed. I had to dig deep to come out of that disappointment. What did I do wrong?

I talked to some of the more experienced teachers like the highly regarded Meneer Esterhuizen, a thoroughbred of the profession, and listened outside his door as he taught his beloved subject, history. It became clear very quickly what I was doing wrong. I taught these students as if they were first-year university students, not high school students with little prior knowledge in the subject. Esterhuizen, I observed, was able to make connections in his teaching between what they already knew and the new material he was introducing. And he did this slowly and systematically, often returning to the two or three key ideas he had chosen to convey. From then on, everything changed and my top students achieved 100 per cent with ease. They were not the problem. I was.

Just as I was beginning to find my rhythm as a new teacher, I came face to face with one of the most unpleasant features of black schooling at the time – the inspector. My subject inspector was the good cop. Mr Schroeder was all *vuur-en-vlam*, this black man who looked white, and sat in my classroom to observe my teaching. Halfway through, he would interrupt and take over the class to show me how to teach a particular concept. I was actually quite pleased with the interruption because I learnt a lot from this experienced biology teacher.

But there was something about how these inspectors intervened that made them the enemy of progressive teachers in the country. They tended to be authoritarian in their manner, like the government for which they worked. They could also be petty in the extreme; it took me a long time to forgive Schroeder for writing down in one of his assessments that I taught without my jacket on. Truly, in a biology class in the heat of the summer, I was judged not for the quality of my teaching or the innovative 'practicals' that I had designed, but because of a damn jacket. I was furious.

These inspectors were also completely blind to the context in which you taught, and could write devastating evaluations about your teaching without any recourse for the teacher observed – as I was about to experience. A panel inspection is when a whole group of inspectors descend on a school to do a thorough evaluation of the institution and its teachers. I was informed that one of them would come and watch me teach music. My objections fell on deaf ears. I had tried to explain that I was teaching music by default.

Earlier in the year, I had walked past a classroom during an interval and noticed that there was a piano in the room. Excited, I sat down and started to play the only thing I knew well – church music and a few awkward classical pieces. At that moment, the principal walked past the empty classroom and promptly announced that I would teach the senior class music. I jumped up and down protesting but Mr Jonker, the principal, insisted: could I at least help out?

There was a music period set aside for each class in the curriculum and there was no specialist music teacher for those slots. I played by ear and had no formal music training of any form whatsoever. Still, I was a member of the team and decided to 'help out', as he put it. Little did I know that there would be a panel inspector to contend with later in the year. The white man sat in my class with a rather glum face as my students sang various spiritual songs that I played on the piano. When I did receive my evaluation report from the inspector, it said that my choice of music was '*eensydig*' (one-sided). I was furious. Music was not my passion, at least not as a formal subject to teach; biology was.

I understood even then why the education department and its inspectors were hated so much, especially in the years following the Soweto Uprising of 1976. I was teaching at Vredenburg in the wake of the Soweto protests (1979 to 1980). You had no voice as a teacher and in this part of rural South Africa, I had little appetite for ethnic politics. I first sensed a cold reaction from some of my colleagues after I was handed forms to complete that would make me part of a coloured teachers' union. I rejected the offer with the contempt it deserved. If I had to be classified, I was a black teacher who did not make a distinction among apartheid's insistent classification of people into 'four racial groups'. I was an outsider because I was English speaking, I was from Cape Town, and I did not join the weekend drinking parties. Still, there was a general respect that we shared as teachers, even though I was definitely not with the 'in group'.

The 1980 student protests, with Cape Town as the epicentre of a post-Soweto movement, challenged the conservatism of this small, rural township of Louwville in Vredenburg. I was extremely proud of my students as they stood up to the brutality of the apartheid regime; several of them spent weeks and longer in prison.

On one occasion, some of the students broke into my little storeroom, taking chemicals and science equipment and causing considerable damage. This would be the first time I encountered a bitter and, for me, still unresolved lesson from student struggles – that the attack on the lab was not personal but an attack on 'the system'. *It's not personal*, student leaders used to tell me many years later as a university principal. But when your own dignity is being trampled on and your family is under attack, that simple reckoning that 'it's not you; it's the system' rings hollow.

After a brief investigation, the department of education took the funds required to replace the equipment from my salary, holding me responsible for the rampage in the store room; the little money that I earned as an unqualified teacher was now even less. I was already on the students' side but this punitive act of a heartless bureaucracy firmed my conviction on the part of the protestors.

It was hard in those days to commit to your passions as a teacher even as you confronted the suppressive politics of education and society. I was starting to find my voice as a teacher activist and ready to call out injustice wherever I saw it. Education and politics were now inextricably tied together in my learning journey as a young teacher. My passion for the one (education) was inevitably my passion for the other (politics).

Now, I was primed to fight and it did not take long for a memorable confrontation with authority. The school informed the matric teachers of opportunities to apply to become sub-examiners for the Standard 10 (now Grade 12) final examinations in our subject area. I applied and was selected. It was an invaluable experience for a new teacher. You learnt from the official 'memorandum of marking' what kinds of answers made sense for particular questions and also where you might have missed the mark in teaching one or other topic.

I was grateful but also angry. I noticed that all the sub-examiners were black but the chief examiner, in charge of the marking of papers from what were then the coloured apartheid schools, was white. I found that difficult to swallow but what pushed me over the edge was that the white schoolboys checking the marks we assigned included the chief's children and their friends – all white. When the marking was over, the man in charge asked our group of about 150 sub-examiners for their feedback on the experience. I raised my hand and said that I found it objectionable that his children and their friends could make holiday money as mark checkers; this was corruption, I suggested, without using the word. I had never seen a white man turn bright red so quickly. He said nothing and dismissed us. When I applied the next year, I was not selected, as expected, and lost a very useful sum of holiday money in the process.

This political consciousness touched every aspect of my professional life as a young teacher. I knew which side I was on. When it came to schools rugby, we could choose to play under the 'Federasie' flag, a group that played 'collaboration-ist' sport with all-white teams, or under 'Saru', the progressive organisation that rallied under the struggle slogan of 'no normal sport in an abnormal society'. In the staff room, the debate was between union membership under the Coloured Cape Teachers Professional Association (CTPA) or independ-ence, until such time that the non-racial Western Cape Teachers Union (WECTU) appeared on the scene in the mid-1980s. Opinion was split and to this day, I find it difficult to embrace those black professionals, whether in rugby, education or poli-tics, who allied with white apartheid organisations for whatever reason. The stakes were high; lives were on the line.

By the time I left Vredenburg for the ruins of District Six, I was more of an activist than when starting out as a teacher. One of the attractions of radical education in the Cape was that there was a very strong tradition in progressive politics that you did not give up education for political struggle. Rather, education was part and parcel of the struggle for liberation. Education was the launch pad for struggle, not something that could be set aside for the broader cause of a free South Africa.

This made intuitive sense to me. The antidote to the poison of 'education for barbarism' (as a celebrated activist by the name of IB Tabata vividly described the evils of apartheid education) was an education that broke the chains of slave education to free the mind and advance the community. I would get a solid education from the moment I arrived at Trafalgar High School in District Six. I was in a school that prided itself on a long struggle history and not a day went by without learning about icons like the poet SV 'Cosmo' Petersen or the advocate Benny Kies among the great teachers of Trafs.

My passion now had a greater cause and, as at Vredenburg, I threw myself into teaching early and late in the day, on weekends and during vacations. I vividly remember two female teachers pass my biology lab as I was beautifying the class: 'New brooms,' said one as they sauntered by. The biology laboratory looked like a bomb had hit it so I decided to remodel the entire place with attractive biological placards, microscopes, working fume cupboards, plant varieties, a small fish tank, and a full human skeleton. The skeleton model looked real to the younger classes so I seized on the opportunity: 'This is what will happen to you if you don't do your homework.' Some students took the warning to heart.

It was at Trafalgar that I witnessed the teaching of some of the best teachers in the world. Mr Emeraan was a truly brilliant mathematics teacher, though I was less impressed with him as a principal–leader; he had a twin brother who was principal of a different high school on the other side of Cape Town and apparently a good physics teacher. Next door to my now thriving biology classroom was another subject master, the physics and chemistry teacher Mr Saleh Adams. We were separated by a shared laboratory room and often I would lean against the door on his side of the lab simply to listen and learn how a maestro teaches science. Saleh was mesmerising as a teacher – and playfully scary: 'My boy, if you don't behave, I will dissolve you in sulphuric acid!' The students loved him and they often got As in this difficult subject in the matric examination. I would tell Saleh over lunch that I eavesdropped on his class and he giggled when I suggested that hydrochloric acid was more potent as a dissolving agent.

If Saleh was my model for passionate teaching then Ernie Steenveld, the deputy principal, was my standard for social commitment. He was an outstanding teacher of English and came from that generation of educators that my friend Crain Soudien included in his book on *The Cape Radicals*. My admiration started when I saw Ernie during one of the breaks sitting in the janitor's closet on the far side of the long corridor that had the principal's office on the other side. Puzzled, I walked over and sat down next to him in the narrow space. Why? He said nothing but I sensed pain and gave him time to decide when he would explain things to me.

One Monday morning, as I came up the steep set of stairs

from the outside gate towards that long corridor where his office was immediately on the left, I noticed that the place was ransacked. Papers were lying everywhere and Ernie stood there picking up the pieces, so to speak. It was the security police. On a regular basis, they would destroy his office, looking for nothing in particular. He was an enemy of the state.

Slowly a story about Mr Steenveld leaked out. In March 1960, when the courageous young UCT student Philip Kgosana, in short pants, led one of the largest anti-pass marches from Langa to Cape Town, the 30 000-strong group came down past the back of the school along De Waal Drive towards the city centre, where they would be confronted by a police force. Ernie was deputy principal at the time and allowed the Trafalgar students to join the swelling march. It was a powerful moment for two reasons: one, it allowed for high school students to join a march of adults; and two, it defied the racial separation of Africans and coloureds in a stand of solidarity that was momentous for its time. Ernie was pursued relentlessly by the apartheid government for his membership of the radical Non-European Unity Movement (NEUM) and his activism in the Teachers' League of South Africa (TLSA).

From that moment on, I developed a deep and abiding respect for Ernie Steenveld for taking a stand against power. I so wish he was alive when De Waal Drive was name Philip Kgosana Drive 23 years after the end of apartheid.

His passion for education and politics was inseparable and it gave direction to my own commitments.

Plough back

I believe that the spirit of giving back is deeply ingrained in the hearts of South African students. In all my leadership positions, I remember students coming to ask for support; to run holiday classes for matric students in their village in northern KwaZulu-Natal. Could I help organise a bus to bring students from schools in the rural Eastern Cape to attend the spectacular Open Days we organised for recruitment purposes on one Saturday per year? There is a particularly smart student in a township school outside Kimberley; could we organise a bursary for her?

Since the time government decided to require students from some disciplines to do a post-qualification service year, as for health sciences students, I was against the idea. You do not force young people to give of their time – you persuade them. In South Africa, I have found that among all youth, black and white, there is a heart for service, an intuitive sense that it is important to give back. For some, this is born out of a sense of mission that comes from a life of faith, but for many, it is out of a sense of obligation – to plough back into their community as a sense of duty.

The beautiful thing about ploughing back is that it is often those who have little to offer who give more, not so much material things as those invaluable gifts of the mind. I know very few university students who come out of hardship who do not use their spare time to teach accountancy or mathematics or after-school drama classes to disadvantaged youth. This is what I sometimes call, borrowing the term from a book of that title by Lisa Dodson, *the moral underground* that keeps our broken country together.

※　　※　　※

The answer was always 'no'. I never thought about living and working in another country. The opportunities came often over the course of my career, both when I started off as a new PhD graduate and when I was established as a scholar in education. Whenever people asked and pointed out that my children were born abroad, and that this was an escape ticket should the need arise, I was offended by such opportunistic reasoning. Grace and my two children, incidentally, are deeply rooted in and committed to South Africa despite their dual citizenship.

This does not mean that there were not times that the thought crossed my mind, especially during the wholesale corruption years of the Zuma administration. But that thought left as fast as it arrived because deep down, there is an unwritten contract that I cannot escape. What I have achieved, however modest, I have to give back to the communities who made my learning possible.

It was not only my parents, but elders in the areas where I grew up, who used this agricultural metaphor to remind us as young people to *plough back into the community*. What this meant for me is that your education is not simply for personal or familial gain; your learning should benefit others beyond the bonds of blood. What this also implied was that learning is not only formal instruction in biology but everyday instruction in life.

That, in a nutshell, is why I do not believe that schools should teach a separate subject called life orientation (LO). It is, for students, a waste of time – in part because it is non-examinable, in the sense that science and maths gets examined, but in part because you cannot contain important values, skills and 'life orientations' within a scheduled period by that name. Let me illustrate.

A teacher who arrives in class before the students and departs only after they leave is teaching life orientation. A teacher who invests in the learning progression of each and every student in her class is conveying an important sense of values and the children will notice it. A teacher who turns around feedback on homework assignments or a test in record time is in fact an LO teacher. A teacher who spends at least five minutes in every class talking up learners who do well and encouraging those who make an effort is a living example of what LO should be conveying to every child.

When you 'box' important generic learning within a low-status subject, you lose all potential for teaching its values. LO, in short, is what every teacher should be doing in the course of teaching the subject, any subject. I tried to do this before the subject was inaugurated in the South African school curriculum.

My students feared the announcement made every year in my register class, the one you are overall responsible for as a teacher: Starting Monday, I will be visiting each one of you in your homes. Tell your parents please. They do not have to prepare anything. I am just coming to visit you as your class teacher.

Trafalgar High School was on the outskirts of the Cape Town city centre, while my home was some distance away in Retreat, which is closer to Muizenberg on the False Bay coastline. It was a good hour's drive one way in peak-hour traffic and my home visits typically ended between 9 and 10 pm at night. Often, I would sleep over at the home of family friends, the Hankeys, in Walmer Estate near the school, where I kept an overnight bag for those evening visitations.

There was one student who pleaded with me not to visit her home. 'Jackie*', I insisted, 'I cannot go to everyone else's home and not yours.' 'Please, sir,' she begged, 'I do not want you to see where or how I live.'

Jackie was a wonderful young student with a proud Afro and forever smile, the decent kind of child who makes you work even harder to ensure they all succeed. By now, I was intrigued about Jackie's determination to keep me away from her home a short drive from the school. When I got to the house, I knew

---

* Not her real name

instinctively what she was afraid of. Jackie and her younger sister, also sporting a smile and an Afro, sat on the steps leading up to the house. There was a mix of sadness and smiles on their faces.

When I got into the house, there was nothing. I mean, nothing. The mother was there but not there, and I suspected alcohol abuse and worse. There was no father, no furniture, and no food. Nothing. I sat on the floor and started to tell the mother what a wonderful student her child was and that I was very proud to have the opportunity to teach her daughter. After some further small talk, I hugged the girls and made my way to the car.

That night I sobbed as I sat in the little white Toyota Corolla outside of the house in Walmer Estate, my overnight accommodation. I was glad I went because now I knew how to teach biology more empathetically. I would teach not only by conveying knowledge, but by ploughing back into the lives of these incredible young people. In that visit, more than any other, I recognised that *learning and living are the same thing.*

Many years later, Jackie called me from the United Kingdom. I had forgotten about her and she needed to remind me who she was and the visit to her home. As she spoke, the emotions came rushing back with the stimulation of memory. Why would she call me after three decades? 'I wanted you to know first,' she said, 'that I obtained my Master's degree.' 'It was all worth it', I told Jackie as we continued talking through the emotion of that wonderful moment of achievement.

Back in Bloemfontein in 2014, I took the short ride from our home in Waverley to the main campus on Nelson Mandela Drive. That trip took me past the east end of the well-known

Mimosa Mall where I would turn right at the traffic lights onto the main road towards the campus gates. Something intrigued me at that right turn. There was always a bunch of middle-aged white men sitting there looking ragged if not also drunk. The obvious question was why on earth these men had not ridden the waves of racial privilege under apartheid where simply showing up with a white skin gave them a tremendous headstart on the majority population?

So one day I stopped my car on the curb at the robots and went to sit with the five men to ask them a simple question: How did you end up here? They were unusually respectful, no doubt recognising the overweight black man as the rector of the university down the road. The local *Volksblad* newspaper made sure I was a regular feature on its pages so it was hard for the locals not to know the rector of Kovsies. The men told me stories of hardship often related to alcohol abuse and a wife who simply could not tolerate the behaviour. And then, as I got up to leave, one of the men said to me in Afrikaans, 'I am a college-trained teacher. I used to teach LO.'

Right there and then, I asked him if he would consider teaching our education students at the university. He was reluctant at first but eventually we made an agreement that he would take one or two classes and see how it went. I contacted HR, who wanted documents a homeless man would not have, so I decided to pay him in cash out of my pocket.

When the first day came, he was all sobered up and I took him to a colleague's class for a lesson on teaching LO. It was the most riveting lecture I had ever experienced. He told the story of his life and then made that simple by asking the students what their assumptions were of the children in their classes. 'Do not ever forget,' he advised these teachers-in-training, 'that the child sleeping in your class might not have eaten last night or slept in a warm bed.' When I dared to look up at the teacher-education students, there were tears in their eyes. This was LO, not from the textbooks but from real life.

My job had no doubt given me privileges that I could leverage to bring a broader education to students. But my salaried occupation also meant that I could use my personal funds to support students in need. I have done this all my life, not for recognition or applause, but because ploughing back is the right thing to do. Sometimes it was a whole bursary for studies at university but often, it has been for smaller amounts of additional funding without which the lack of money for toiletries or transport could become the straw that breaks the camel's back – and the student drops out.

Ploughing back means being alert to and aware of the needs of those around you, and for me that often meant students at school or university. One particularly visible adventure was the No Student Hungry (NSH) campaign that we launched at UFS. A small research project on campus showed that almost 60 per cent of our students were food insecure. This meant that they did not know where their next meal would come from. So we started to raise private funding to feed those students three times a day. I started the fund by donating all the royalties of one of my earlier popular books, *We Need to Talk*, to the fund. That was about R100 000 and a good start to the effort. Companies and individuals donated generously. Some of my staff walked from Bloemfontein to Cape Town as a fundraiser and were met on the grounds of the famous St George's Cathedral by an amazing partner in the project, Archbishop Thabo Makgoba. Poor students graduated, always mentioning the difference that food support made in their learning and their lives.

But what made NSH different from being simply another social welfare intervention was that it required the student recipients to plough back. They had to commit to a particular community project as part of their service learning and were constantly reminded that when they were on their feet one day, to do the same for students in need. The term 'paying it forward' became well-known at this time. The plan worked and the implementers of the programme, led by the spouses of the Rector (Grace) and the Dean of Students (Carin Buys), who also served as a volunteers, were able to embed the values of selflessness and service in the lives of the beneficiaries of the NSH.

Ploughing back does not, however, only mean the distribution of money. It also involves the sharing of expertise, the lending of support, advising in difficult learning journeys, and that simple capacity to be available on the other side of a telephone or an email account. One of the most fulfilling ways in which I tried to plough back was to visit what now must number hundreds of schools around the nine provinces of South Africa. True, while at UFS I went with the additional goal of recruiting top students, from 'Maritzburg to Mokopane, yet my message (singular) to any assembly of students contained the same basic ingredients shared in this book.

I start by making the point that *you are smarter than you think*. You are even smarter than some of your teachers or relatives might think. And you are smarter than the government thinks. Why else would we have a 30 and 40 per cent pass in school subjects and a subject called life orientation? And why are so many of you doing mathematical literacy? It is not because you're dumb, but because you were taught poorly, and somewhere in the lower grades, you developed a negative attitude towards maths and that is why you're doing a subject that will not get you into most university courses and degrees. There is nothing wrong with you. The entire system thinks you're not smart enough.

When I say these kinds of things, the students become very excited. They know the truth, that they are being short-changed by the system; the standard for passing the National Senior Certificate is not that rigorous but passing at university is a completely different story. Some teachers are usually less excited about my talks, especially those doing LO and mathematical literacy. Some of them understand the broader point that I am making and are prepared to coast along with the generalisations. Others take the criticism very personally; at one East London school, the teachers were so angry they would not greet me afterwards. At a Pretoria school, a teacher wrote me a long letter laced with personal insults. Mostly, though, the goal of the talks – to inspire students to aim higher – was well-understood by school teachers.

Two schools would not have me address the students. The one was York High School in George and the other was a private school in Rondebosch. Both schools had their preferred university to work with, Stellenbosch in the case of York and UCT for the Rondebosch school. It was, however, clear to me that there was a filthy snobbery at work as well – UFS was, for some of these people, a rural Afrikaans university in the backwoods of central South Africa. Fortunately, the students from these institutions knew better and we were always able to recruit some young people from the elite high schools in every province and not only into the sought-after disciplines of medicine and architecture.

Ploughing back also means telling the truth. And in this respect, I was especially hard on the elite white schools where the teachers were still almost all white, the learners majority white, and the school culture and extracurriculum activities white in every sense. These too are our children and my message to them was direct: *I am sure your school will provide you with competent teaching in science and mathematics; what I am not sure about is whether your school will teach you the decency required to be a competent citizen in a new South Africa.*

In these moments, the auditorium would fall silent. We were now talking about race and racial privilege. These are uncomfortable topics for South Africans. I would make myself vulnerable in these situations with biographical snippets of my own struggles with race. This normally makes it easier for audiences to open up. I would also inject some humour at just the right points in these difficult conversations so as to make it easier for the message to carry. It took years to refine this delivery in ways that keeps the attention of the audience and at the same time locks in the message about racial justice. Most times, it works.

The hard reality is that the elite schools of South Africa do a good job of narrow academic preparation and a less stellar job of preparing students to live and learn in an unjust world. Boys' schools are particularly weak when it comes to talking about and acting on issues of racial privilege and social injustice. I was very lucky to be able to team up with teacher activists Roy Hellenberg and Dylan Wray to put together a multimedia resource for such schools called *A School Where I Belong* that deals with issues such as unconscious bias in a very practical and systematic way.

It is a duty of service that I regard as important since my work in turnaround projects has focused on that 80 per cent of our schools stuck in disadvantage and decay. To be sure, some of the elite schools are open to the broader message of transformation and the real issues of inclusion when it comes to black teachers being appointed and more black students being enrolled. But the situation is very complex, as my doctoral student Samantha Kriger and I point out in a book titled *Who Gets in and Why: Race, class and aspiration in South Africa's elite schools* (2020). For reasons of history and politics, the white elite schools will remain predominantly white in composition and culture, with a small but visible presence of mainly black middle-class students. This, we find, is the result of an unspoken political settlement between the white and black elites, where the racial interests of whites and the class interests of blacks converge to sustain this minority of privileged schools in post-apartheid South Africa.

Where I do spend most of my time ploughing back, however, is in the majority of our schools, which are black (broadly speaking) and under-resourced, whether in the urban townships like Langa in Cape Town or the rural areas of Thohoyandou in Limpopo. I realised some time ago that it was very difficult turning around struggling institutions given the sheer scale of the problem – 26 000 schools. So I recruited an American filmmaker, Molly Blank (mentioned earlier), and composed the book *How to Fix South Africa's Schools* (2014). We got a generous funder and placed this book with 18 spectacular videos on DVD inside every high school in South Africa. It was a distillation of research from 'schools that work' in difficult contexts, together with video-documentaries of two top black schools in each province, where the goal was to capture what made these schools exceptional in an ecology of deprivation.

The general factors that made certain disadvantaged schools excel were confirmed in this documentary study – strong principal leadership, competent teachers and parental involvement in the work of the schools. Except – you cannot 'copy and paste' the successes of one school onto another, for a simple reason: every school has its own culture. That culture is reflected in the social history of the school, the politics of the various school actors and the status of the school in the community. Culture, that sense of 'this is how we do things around here', is something that is hard to change. And yet you could ask, what among the many variables in educational research is the one factor most likely to turn a school around? That answer is easy – a competent and committed school principal. Leadership matters more than anything else in mobilising the other elements (like worn-out teachers) behind a compelling vision.

And so I crossed the land, visiting troubled schools and trying to plough back, using the skills I now had and the experiences I had accumulated by studying schools in different countries. One of the hard lessons I had to confront in my learning journey is how often things do not work out as planned, despite the investment of resources. Once again, it helped to budget for emotional disappointment. Two contrasting cases from Bloemfontein come to mind.

Since my expertise lies with high schools, I was always reluctant to take on primary schools but the principal of this school asked for help so my team showed up. They needed the basic infrastructure of this dilapidated school to be upgraded. We raised the funds from the private sector with supporting funds from the provincial government of the Free State. The team built a state-of-the-art library and remodelled the pre-school education facilities on the site. An impressive fence was built to prevent theft and easy access by criminal elements. A date was set for a visit by some top funders from Johannesburg.

On the day of arrival, I was shocked and embarrassed. The school looked like a pigsty. Books lay spread all over the so-called library. Dirt stood in heaps around the place. And they had known the date and time of the visit by the dignitaries. After the show was over, I returned alone the next day and called for a staff meeting. I made it clear that the school lacked leadership and that the only way change would happen is if they became active as change agents in their own schools (a topic raised often before), rather than simply expecting precious resources to be dropped into the school. That said, I told the staff we were ending the project right there and then. You can only plough back in fertile soil.

This is a hard lesson to learn and to share but let me say this. One of the main reasons for the persistence of dysfunction in our schools has less to do with apartheid and much to do with the lack of energy, initiative, drive and determination on the part of school actors – the principal, teachers, parents and, yes, the provincial department of education. If your school is dirty, pick up the damn litter. If your science classroom lacks attractive charts and diagrams, then beg or borrow or buy some and put them up. If your learners are habitually late, close the gate at 7.30 am and start teaching regardless. This is not a policy matter. Nor is this political intrigue. It simply means that dedicated leaders and teachers do what they are paid to do. *Show up and plough back*. Which of course raises the question: Why does this not happen?

Simple. It is other people's children. After years of Toyota's investment in primary school education, mainly in the areas where their employees' children attend school, the company's CEO sat with us as we pondered the question: Why is government so indifferent to the fate of black schools? What prompted the question was yet another drowning of a little child in a pit latrine, with his arm stretched beyond the muck, desperately searching for a hand to lift him out. Dryly, the CEO said in one sentence what eludes libraries of educational research on the topic: They just don't care.

Ploughing back, in this perspective, is not about bringing skills and competences to bear on a troublesome problem, whether in education or healthcare or the provision of housing. It is, deep down, about a set of values. If you fix a school simply because of the tender contract, you would have done your job and the terms of the contract between government and service provider would have been duly honoured. But how often does the contractor take the money and run without any building? Or do the job halfway, then disappear? Or do the job, but part of the roof or the foundation of the building collapses soon afterwards because of cheap materials, not what was required in the specs?

When this happens, the problem is not technical competence but one of basic values, where the commitment goes beyond fulfilling the terms of the contract to the understanding that this is for the children of the community and I will do my best to deliver the best building in the shortest time possible. They simply do not care.

The black elites do not care because their children are in the former white schools. Show me one member of parliament whose children attend township schools. Show me an academic or business personality whose children attend classes in the African languages. Show me a member of the dominant teachers' union whose children attend a school that is regularly disrupted by that union. It does not happen because it is other people's children, not their own, affected by disruption and dysfunction.

To plough back is not a legal obligation or something that should result from a sense of guilt. It is something you do out of a deep and happy sense of duty, precisely because you have been given much that can be shared for the benefit of others.

On the other side of Bloemfontein was a school with the misleading name of Headstart. It did nothing of the sort. The school was a cheap, private alternative for someone willing to make a quick buck off the meagre earnings of the poor. As a result, children who did not get into the mainstream public schools, either because they were poor foreign nationals without papers or repeat failures, would end up at Headstart. The principal of the school came to see me at the university and pleaded for help.

I went over there and the school was a mess. The infrastructure was crumbling and the classes, when learners attended, were overloaded. Teachers came and went because salary payments were completely unpredictable, given that half the students could not afford fees in the first place.

Shortly afterwards, I asked for a meeting with the teachers, parents and learners, and the place was packed. I said that the university could help the school but that there were conditions like full attendance by learners, and teaching in every single period by the teachers. We provided extra teacher resources and the plan went into operation. I taught the first period English class to the matriculants once a week alongside the regular teacher. Halfway through this experiment, I realised that the finances of the school were in a shambles and that there was possible corruption.

I asked to see the owner, who came bouncing into my office in an unprofessional manner. It was difficult to suppress my anger and I made it clear that her conduct and attire were unacceptable in a professional setting and that somebody from my office would immediately do an investigation into the finances of the school.

Because of the dedicated teaching resources we put into the school, Headstart had its highest-ever pass rate that year and several of the students were invited to study at UFS free of charge. Some of them obtained their degrees. Here, once again, I had discovered a powerful lesson about children, which is worth emphasising.

From time to time, I am asked to teach in a special global seminar at one of the most prestigious institutions in the world, a private girls' school in California. In any given year, I would, on invitation, teach a few classes in township schools in South Africa. I often think about and compare the children I taught in that wealthy school in Palo Alto and those in a township school like Zwelethemba in Worcester. Here is the honest truth: there is absolutely no difference between the US children and the SA children. They all reveal incredible talent; they all can be drawn out into courageous conversations; they all have the capacity to ask deep and probing questions. The only difference between these two schools and the children who inhabit them is *the structure of opportunity*.

In other words, given the same opportunities, all children can achieve the same standards of learning. It is still one of the foundational references for my work with schools, the famous dictum of the Harvard psychologist Jerome Bruner: 'We begin with the hypothesis that any subject can be taught in some intellectually honest form to any child at any stage of development.' It wasn't much of a hypothesis to be tested because Bruner added quickly: 'No evidence exists to contradict it; considerable evidence is being amassed that supports it.'

But who does the teaching, with what kind of resources and in what contexts are the kind of questions that matter in making sense of Bruner's hypothesis in South African schools. The point is, the problem is not the learners. It is the structured opportunities that make effective teaching and powerful learning possible for all children. If every policy was designed and every plan executed with this basic understanding in mind, the learning possibilities for every child would be truly limitless.

This commitment to ploughing back has its roots in my family upbringing. I was really fortunate to have parents, Abraham (Abie) and Sarah (Sally), who lived their lives sacrificially. My mother, a nurse who worked tirelessly in an orthopaedic hospital in day- and nightshifts would still come home to clean and cook for the extended family as if she were a full-time homemaker. And yet in every spare second she would knit jerseys or stitch clothing together for 'the less privileged'. My dad, far more laid back than his wife, had this urge to do mission work in the upcountry areas, where he preached the gospel and delivered food and clothing every other weekend.

That sense of mission had a profound influence on me, and so from my student years, I would, alone or with friends, hitchhike from Cape Town to Strydenburg (a small town near the white state of Orania and on the road towards Kimberley) to serve the people during the week and convene church services on Sundays. One of my tasks was to transfer women patients in the bakkie of a senior church elder from Strydenburg to Hopetown every Friday night. Men would return from the farms on weekends. They would drink themselves into a stupor and then beat their wives. I was the one-man ambulance, taking these poor women for treatment at the nearest hospital. It was truly heartbreaking and I often asked the women that silly question bereft of sociological understanding: 'Why don't you just leave him?' One day, I got an answer the meanings of which I still grapple with today: 'I will worry when he stops beating me because then he probably has another woman.'

What I have learnt about ploughing back is that it truly is more blessed to give than to receive. That when you give, not out of abundance, but sacrificially, then you never really are stranded with nothing. That a selfish life is a joyless life for in ploughing back, your own life is not only enriched but given purpose and meaning. And that in giving of yourself, not simply your resources, living and learning come together in perfect unison.

Keep your feet on the ground

I had never met a Ms Anything before, let alone a Miss South Africa who became Miss World. Rolene Strauss was a medical student at my university, and long before she won the big beauty competitions, I had occasion to meet the tall young woman from the small rural town of Vryburg few South Africans would have known about, let alone visited. A test-tube baby, born to nurse-and-doctor parents, Rolene made an impression because of her humility before and after greatness. In my community, they would call such people down to earth.

I have never been a fan of beauty competitions but I became one for Rolene, especially when she called me one night and asked that I please come '*met Mevrou*' ('with Mrs', the tactful Afrikaans university language for the rector's wife) to see her compete for the 2011 Miss South Africa title. I really did not feel like driving the long distance from Bloemfontein to Sun City but this was my student and so *Mevrou* and I hit the road. One of the judges came over to our table and whispered to me that the title was hers to lose.

Unfortunately, towards the end of the competition, the big question that each candidate must answer stumped my beautiful student. How could you ask an Afrikaans lass from Vryburg whether beauty competitions were becoming, wait for it, 'blasé'? She stumbled and everyone knew it was over.

Next thing I knew, Rolene was back in my office on campus. Losing must have hurt but she was as calm as she was determined. I am taking the year off, Prof, and then will try again after that. Well, as they say, the rest is history.

At her wedding in 2016 on a beautiful farm in Somerset West, she alighted like a princess from a horse-drawn carriage. As Miss World 2014 went around the wedding venue, greeting her guests, it was crystal clear to me that this was still that little girl from Vryburg with her feet planted firmly on the ground.

*   *   *

The flies on the bowl of porridge in front of me looked like raisins stuck to the sugary lumps on the surface. I stared in horror at what this poor family had put on the table and I regretted making the trip to this upcountry town with my mission-inspired father. I was about 10 or 11 years old and becoming very conscious of self and image at this stage. No ways. I am not eating this thick porridge with the flies all over it and far too little milk to begin with.

Off to the side sat my father, a gentle man who normally would not force the issue. But he knew the people of the house were watching and that what was at stake was not the porridge but whether this family from Cape Town with their own car would deign to eat what was on the table. As I drew back from the porridge, my eye caught my father's; he was dead serious, the normally jocular Abie. And then with a firm but subtle nod of the head, I knew it was over. I had no choice but to eat the porridge.

Of course, there was a much larger lesson of living and learning that my father was communicating. You might be a lower-middle-class family from Cape Town but these are farm-workers with nothing to offer but porridge in the mid-morning. Even disadvantage has its gradations. Come down from what-ever your perch is. Share the meal with the family. It was a lesson I never forgot.

As the qualifications came, the awards and the honours, and the serious professional appointments at home and abroad, I always remembered that bowl of porridge. Never think highly of yourself. Keep your feet solidly on the ground. It helped enormously that my parent's faith instilled that language of humility in all their children, something that lends meaning to my life to this day. Whatever you have is not your own; it is a consequence of grace upon your life. Pride comes before a fall. Count others more important than yourself. This was not only sound Biblical wisdom; it is good common sense as well.

That bowl of porridge would stay with me through my career, particularly one memorable day on the west coast. I was doing my usual home visits to students in my register class at the Vredenburg school. This Saturday morning took me to Laaiplek on the coast, a pleasant drive on the well-tarred R399 in my first car, a yellow Ford Cortina. At the student's home, I was warmly welcomed and invited to sit at a solidly wooden table in the kitchen. As in Jackie's house, there was nothing much in the kitchen except a bottle of wine. The father, a tall and sturdy fisherman, brought out two glasses and promptly poured me a large drink.

This was a problem for two reasons. I had never drunk wine in my life and I also had to make the drive back to Vredenburg after the visit. This was all the man could offer and he worked with the comfortable assumption that, like every man in that part of the world, 'real men', I enjoyed the fruit of the vine.

So I drank the glass of wine as slowly as possible but when the fisherman offered a refill I made some excuse about having to be back at school. How I survived the return trip to Vredenburg I do not know. All I remember is that the car swerved all over the road and that I pulled off once or twice to try and regain my vision and focus. It was frightening in part because of the new-ness of the experience and because I did not know when I would get back full control of my senses. Thankfully, I arrived safely at the hostel and slept through the night. I realised afterwards that two personal commitments were in dangerous conflict – the desire to respect the family and a life of abstinence. I would certainly never recommend drinking and driving.

When your feet are not on the ground, it is easy to get carried away by the positive things people say about you in private and on public platforms. You need to learn quickly how to deal with praise and flattery, and the very thin line between these two forms of adulation. Sometimes people mean well and there is a genuine word of recognition in the praise. At other times, the nice words are meant to get something from you or worse. Whatever the motivation of the speaker, receive the positive words gracefully and always seek to deflect the kindness towards others.

Here are some examples of worthwhile sharing of the honours. Your outstanding research team, without which the new book, though you are the primary author, would never have seen the light of day. The secretary who made all the arrangements behind the scenes, without which you might not have made the speaking appointment in time. Your editor, whose hard work and guidance made the book a much better professional product. The two friends who read earlier drafts of the article and made invaluable comments before the manuscript was accepted by this leading international journal.

The nice thing about *academic deflection* in favour of others is that it is true. None of us produces work of any kind – whether it is research for publication or the company's annual financial statements or the landing of a plane – without the technical assistance and advice from a host of co-workers. And when you routinely praise others, you gain the respect of those whom you are privileged to lead. Who would forget that stunning research finding about leaders in Jim Collins's *Good to Great*, that exceptional leaders have a strong sense of moral purpose and deep sense of personal humility?

Keeping your feet on the ground means seeing your success in perspective. During the many graduation ceremonies over which I was required to preside, there were always a few moments at the end when the vice-chancellor was called on to make closing remarks. At every ceremony, I would ask the graduates to stand, turn towards the rafters, and acknowledge the people who brought them there. I would remind the students that there was a grandmother who used her pension money to contribute towards registration costs, a parent who took on loans to pay off outstanding fees, a sibling who postponed studies so that the financial burden on the family was lessened, a spouse who worked doubly hard to take care of the children so that the partner could study late into the night. In other words, I would rightly remind my students that *you did not get here on your own.*

At the back of my mind is the inescapable truth that throughout my years of overseas study, my wife Grace was the one person who made it possible for me to study without financial stress. She worked on both campuses, first as a computer analyst at Cornell and then as the manager of a thriving daycare centre (and manager of the activities for graduate families). That brought in vital complementary dollars that supported our two blessings, Mikhail born in New York and Sara-Jane born in California. Without her role, financially and emotionally, I would not have survived the stresses of being a student at competitive research universities. I did not get anywhere on my own.

This acknowledgement – that the support of others is key to anyone's success – brings us back to the question that started this reflection on my learning journey. What explains the fact that two children raised by the same family in the same home with the same advantages or disadvantages can follow two completely different paths? The one becomes a neurosurgeon and the other a drunk, the one famously wealthy and the other a hobo living on the streets.

I do know a few things from my observations. I have learnt that it is important not to judge the one who appears to have achieved less. Fate can deal one sibling an unexpected knock, such as the death of a child, from which that parent never recovers, or the unexpected loss of a good job or an addiction that was never conquered. This can happen to anyone and no person dares stand in judgement.

What I also know is that for those deemed successful, by any measure, they did not get there by themselves. Once again, those 'what if?' questions come back to haunt me.

What if there was no Paul Galant or Archie Dick or Uncle Martin or Chabani Manganyi? What if I was born into a home where my parents were alcoholics and without the spiritual wisdom or emotional security that they provided us as children? The answer to such questions can only lead towards the path of gratitude, which plants one's feet firmly on the ground. You act in relation to such grace.

This is exactly what happened when I landed at the University of the Free State in 2009. It was merely months after that horrible tragedy had occurred when four white male students had racially abused five black workers. The more I studied the situation, the more I realised that the institution was also at fault, even if they tried to pass off the crime as the result of 'four bad apples' in an otherwise innocent university. Along with the society in which they grew up (home, church, peer groups, cultural associations, sport affiliations), this former-white university with its conservative values had made those students into what they had become. The criminal and civil courts would have their say on the matter but what about the university's response beyond the decision, before my arrival, to suspend the students from further studies?

I thought about this hard and long, and discussed possible responses with black and white leaders on and off campus. It was clear to me that the university could serve as a platform for a much broader and deeper resolution of the tragedy. On the occasion of my inauguration as vice-chancellor, I decided to announce a decision that we had discussed and which I would elaborate on that evening. I would take responsibility for what had happened. Of course, I was not there at the time of the incident, nor was I a white South African. It did not matter. I was the head of the institution and in that capacity, I took ownership of and responsibility for the event. Drawing on a deep reserve of spirituality seeded by my parents and the community in which I grew up, I explained the decision in this way at the inaugural event: *I can forgive because I have been forgiven.*

Not long after, across the small coffee table in my office sat the head of one of the major black unions in the province, a huge man with an unsmiling face. What gave him added stature in politics was that he carried the name of one of the young heroes of the anti-apartheid struggle from the time of the

Soweto Uprisings. He was aware of the significance of the family name. What this political leader wanted was unmitigated reprisals meted out to the four 'boys', as he called them. I told him about the courts. No, he also wanted the university to make sure they never studied on this campus again. I explained that the students were remorseful and considering asking forgiveness and paying reparation. None of that washed with the powerful unionist. They should pay. At that point, I leaned forward and asked him, softly, Mr Mashinini, have you ever done anything wrong? Did you ever desire forgiveness? He went quiet and did not respond. The meeting was over.

There is an ugly truth about great achievers in our society. Not everyone knows how to handle fame and fortune. We all know the gangster with his ill-gotten gains who flings money from the back of his limousine as old and young scurry to pick up the cash. Time after time I have seen prominent black achievers, the first in their families, treat their staff with disdain, silence opposition, marginalise groups they disagree with and boast openly about their achievements. Sometimes it gets quite ridiculous with the availability of social media where prominent leaders boast of new hairstyles or six-pack lovers or travels abroad. Such are the actions of insecure and immature people who simply do not know how to receive their gifts graciously and to be conscious, always, of those still struggling to make it in learning as in life.

Keeping your feet on the ground, therefore, means that your significance as a human being lies not in external attributions placed upon you but in *who you are as a person*. The academic who insists on being called 'professor' and throws a hissy fit when someone makes the mistake of calling him 'doctor' relies for his sense of wholeness on a ridiculous title. The politician or businessman who keeps a temporary, honorary title because of a period appointment as 'professor' at some university is not only dishonest but also desperate for regard.

The school that makes a fuss about the hair dress of black girls or boys conveys a message that your worth lies in the extent to which you comply with some arcane rule carried down over generations of students. These are colonial hang-ups from our past that misplace value in dress or degrees.

When are you going to upgrade your car? I got that question more than once from my students. For years, I drove the same old Pajero with its battered frame from Pretoria to Bloemfontein to Cape Town. There were two reasons I held onto that car. It worked and it was unpretentious. When I went to do work in township schools, I felt comfortable. There was no need to show off. My sense of self had nothing to do with the model of car I was driving. That is why I was shattered when a man went through a red traffic light in Bridgetown in the Cape and knocked my poor Pajero to smithereens. 'Did you not see the light was red?' I asked the young Mozambican. 'I know, but I was coming.' I was forced to buy another car.

The power of recognising such inward value means that you are not intimidated by the external parade of authority. Nothing demonstrated this more beautifully than when Nelson Mandela was in the dock during the 1963–64 Rivonia Trial. It was literally a life-or-death moment. Judge Quartus de Wet no doubt was dressed up in the heavy gowns of judicial authority with equally appropriate dress for the prosecutor seeking the death penalty, Percy Yutar, in the splendour of the misnamed Palace of Justice. All very intimidating. Then Mandela spoke in his defence. After introducing himself as the first accused, Madiba said this: 'I hold a Bachelor's degree in Arts and practised as an attorney in Johannesburg for a number of years in partnership with Oliver Tambo.'

I have thought long and hard why, of all the things he could have started with, Nelson Mandela would have mentioned his qualification and his profession. It might have been custom among the gentlemanly class but I like to think it was something deeper that motivated the great leader. The degree mattered because it was not only something he worked hard for; it was something the state with its awesome powers of life and death could not take away from him. His profession mattered because whatever transpired in that court, he had the knowledge with which to understand, engage and even refute whatever judgement the court might bring.

Anyone who knew Madiba, even from a distance, would understand that this was no idle boast. He was not a boastful person. He was merely making sure that the judge and his company understood what he had within him – a quiet confidence of knowledge and a relevance of experience that could not be denied. This is what the achievement of knowledge enables in the grounded person – a self-assurance that enables one to confront even the most difficult situations with a calm and confidence that speaks of conviction rather than conceit. The future statesman's feet were firmly on the ground.

What Nelson Mandela's example also demonstrates is that *humility is certainly not timidity*. In the course of my learning journey, I have come to understand how important it is to use one's knowledge in the public arena too, to take a stand against what is wrong. It saddens me that those who took a bold stand against the apartheid government, often risking their lives, would melt away in the face of a venal and corrupt post-apartheid government.

No public position offers a more powerful platform that that of the university vice-chancellor. Few of these leaders use that opportunity to speak out against government interference in higher education or the destructive violence of student politics or corruption within the state. Except for personalities like Adam Habib from Wits University or Saleem Badat from Rhodes University, academic leaders at this level are remarkably silent from one crisis to the next. Many turn inwards, fearful of standing up and speaking out on public issues that affect education.

That timidity is even worse in the civil service, where obsequiousness toward ministers and other higher-ups has been developed into a fine art. The fawning in public view is unbelievable with the result that these ministers and deputies, who once were low-level activists hidden from public view, begin to believe that the sleek black cars with blue-light convoys, the red carpets and praise singers, really do mean that they are important persons. My late mother had a sharp rebuke when observing these kinds of peacocks in our community: '*Dis wat gebeur as niks iets word!*' (This is what happens when nothing becomes something.)

These are the kinds of people who fight to the death (often literally, as in some of the provinces) to hold on to these positions, for without these jobs, many of them are unemployable, with no real skills or competences to survive in the real world. They become boastful on public platforms and comically assert that they have powers not available to the ordinary man or woman. They can pick up the rand when it falls. They know more about Aids than the medical scientists. They can shop during a coronavirus lockdown. They are above not only the laws of nature but also the laws they themselves make.

As an education activist, for me, keeping your feet on the ground means telling authorities the truth about misleading matric results, about children who drown in pit latrines and about the destructive roles of the powerful teachers' union allied with the ruling party. To be a public nuisance is, for me, a public duty. The problem is when you stand alone, then you stand out and the vile ones among them will come for you, disregarding the importance of critical voices in a democratic society. It is not that the vile ones disagree with you for purposes of extending the debate; it is that they come for you personally to break you down so as not to shed light on a public concern.

Not infrequently, somebody will ask the question: How do you withstand the constant attacks on you? Here again, I have benefited from my mother's wisdom which I outlined, with my sister Naomi, in the book *Song for Sarah* (2017). What helps me through a torrent of criticism is the conviction that what I have said is true. Once I have the evidence to prove an argument – such as the declining standards of the matric exam – then nothing that the minister or her officials say can intimidate me. If what you believe is right, my mother would say, then you have nothing to fear; the truth is on your side and you can sleep easily at night.

But there is another thing that helps one weather bad press. It is that you are never alone in difficult situations. Perhaps the most emotional reaction I have ever had to a difficult situation was when Julius Malema and his comrades announced that they would pay me a visit for the Reitz decision regarding the four racist students. The media licked their lips and were camped on Die Rooiplein (The Red Square) outside my office from early that morning.

I, too, was in the office early to start work and prepare my senior management team for the visit of the men, and our media office for the inevitable surge of news that would come out of the visit. My colleagues were supportive but I could sense a measure of dread. This event was billed as high noon on the Kovsie campus. I was concerned for my family and the team. I worried about what this would mean for the university and whether we were adequately equipped in the event of a riot.

At that moment, just before 7 am, my secretary came through the interleading door from her office, holding a message on a small piece of white paper. Her head down, she read what she had scribbled from the phone-call. In Afrikaans, she shared the following: A *boer* (farmer) had called from a small farming town in the rural Free State. He wanted the rector to know that he should not worry about the visit by Mr Malema. The whole farm had gathered in the barn that evening, the farmer, his family and all the workers, and they had prayed through the night for the rector. I must be calm. It will be okay.

Before Ilse had come to the end of the message, I was already choked up. Think about it, I told myself, this is a man and a community whom I had never met, and who had absolutely no reason to be concerned about me, let alone pray through the night for a stranger. And the obvious fact was not lost on me that the farmer was white and the rector was black. Instantly, I knew, the meeting with the firebrand leader of the youth league of the ruling party was in good hands. As is now widely known, the meeting ended peacefully and productively, as the farmer and the community had prayed for. The crowd dispersed quietly. The reconciliation process would proceed.

If I did not already believe, that day I would have.

Feet on the ground, some have asked: How effective is the role of the critic in the public arena? This is an important question. It would be rather futile making a lot of noise in the social, print and other media (radio, television) without any effect. Over time, however, one becomes conscious of how your messages reach the powerful. Several of my former postgraduate students work in the Union Buildings and have told me how they'd dreaded Thursdays – that was the day my column in *The Times* would appear and force discussion on the issue raised that week. I do know from good authority that government eventually reformed and then ditched Outcomes Based

Education because of relentless criticism by our research team going back to the first comprehensive analysis of this damaging policy in my paper, 'Ten reasons why OBE will fail'. It took a long time and three ministers before this political project was eventually discarded but the negative consequences are still evident in schools to this day.

Of course, no minister has the humility to acknowledge openly that external criticism of one or other education policy led to the abandonment of the idea. That is too much to ask of the high and mighty. They would castigate you even as they listened to you. Only one minister understood the necessary role of criticism in a democracy and development and she would regularly ask me to assist in restoring governance and management at one or other university, or building a new cohort of young professors for the South African academy. She got much heat from her colleagues for bringing me in and at one stage had to disinvite me from an official assignment because 'the social cluster' of ministers was dead set against my involvement in trying to rebuild education. It was and still is a sign of the immaturity of our democracy.

Kader Asmal, the fiery second Minister of Education, had an ambivalent relationship with me as critic. An academic himself, Kader understood the importance of critics and dissent in a democracy. But he had an extra-large ego and just enough of an authoritarian streak to deal swiftly with his enemies. It was more than amusing when as Education Minister, this legal scholar called me, an education man, a charlatan; my friends had a lot of fun with that. He was also sly as a fox.

A day or two before the matric examination results were to be released, Kader would call for a friendly chat. How are you, Jonathan? I did not know him on a first-name basis and the first time it happened, I was puzzled. Then the penny dropped. Kader was hoping I would be soft in my criticism of the results, which jumped dramatically (and erroneously) during his reign. The minister soon learnt that he was wasting his time with such a cheap political stunt. I would discover after his death that Kader was asked to consider working with me.

Tony Heard won recognition in ANC circles for publishing in the *Cape Times*, of which he was editor, a 1985 interview he conducted in London with the banned ANC leader, Oliver Tambo. Heard was promptly charged under the much-abused Internal Security Act. He was also Kader's adviser and in his book, *8000 Days* (2019), he shares these reflections about 'the freezing out of talent' in relation to my relationship with the Minister of Education:

> I once found myself sitting next to Jansen when I was deputising for an unavoidably absent Kader Asmal at a dinner in Durban. I was treated to a potted tutorial on education. It was obvious that Jansen knew his subject and had much to offer. I mentioned my feelings about Jansen on my return to Pretoria. I picked up an inexplicable disconnect between these two brilliant minds. During this period, and beyond, Jansen was to be a severe critic on various subjects and seemed locked out of being a useful influence on government. He could

have been a critical but constructive ally if treated with more sensitivity and respect by the politicians.

I found this unusually honest account of political behaviour to be less a point about a politician and a professor, and more about the state of our country and the incapacity to recognise the value of critical voices in democracy and development.

Parting thoughts

The annual camp for Christian students was at hand. I dropped my daughter early that morning for the bus trip departing from the UFS campus. It was still dark but this was one of those rare opportunities for the rector to meet parents dropping off their children. So I went around to the fancy SUVs, shaking hands – until I got to this battered car and approached the two white parents. The father gave me a stiff handshake but then his wife took off running.

What nonsense was this? Apartheid was over. She might not be comfortable with me as a black person but it was time to get over our divisions.

So I ran after the woman and caught up with her. 'What are you scared of?' I asked the woman with hands on her knees. 'Are you okay?'

'Yes,' she said. 'I just didn't want the rector to see me in my dressing gown.'

* * *

The most challenging lesson in the course of my learning journey has been finding a way of dealing with my bitterness about the past in relation to white South Africans. Of Jacques Delors' four pillars of education (learning to know, learning to do, learning to be), I found the fourth one the most difficult – learning to live together. After more than a century of racial segregation, how do you simply show up at the end of apartheid and embrace those who stole your property, humiliated your parents, uprooted your family, imprisoned your people and stifled your education?

As a young man, I was embittered until several things helped me make sense of my pain. I heard about Beyers Naudé and Bram Fischer, white men from the Afrikaner brotherhood who paid a great price for standing up against apartheid. My heart opened up after hearing of the hanging of John Harris and the assassination of David Webster for their courage in the struggle. I came to understand how the very idea of 'congress politics' was premised on the notion of our common humanity and that the struggle was against a system of evil, not random individuals. Oliver Tambo, a man of deep faith, made a deep and lasting impression on me as I struggled with my racial demons.

Then I started to teach and lead white students at the University of Pretoria, and my heart opened forever. I was now an advocate for racial reconciliation even as abiding memory kept lurking in the background. I was determined to reach out to my white brothers and sisters with all the courage that took.

I can give a long list of friends and acquaintances who have been destroyed by this riptide of racial anger and resentment.

They fit in nowhere, constantly on the edge and angry. I understand and will never judge them. The only problem is that racial bitterness eats away at your soul and caps your ambitions. Frankly, you become a victim twice. It is a hard but necessary choice to patiently and determinedly swim back against this powerful, debilitating current. When you do, there are lighter moments that help carry you to shore.

This short memoir of my learning journey is intended to inspire and give direction; to share ideas and suggest resources; to warn of pitfalls and encourage sacrifice. If even one student finds her or his path from these lessons in life and learning, then writing this book will have been worth it.